D0461401

From the Library of

DAVE WATSON

B267 © Jon Brett Studio, Inc.

THE BATTLE OF BRITAIN
MEMORIAL FLIGHT

The Inside Story of The Royal Air Force Memorial Flight

Ripping

Ripping Publishing
PO Box 286
Epsom, Surrey,
England KT19 9YG

ISBN 1 899884 01 7

Printed by Butler & Tanner Ltd, Frome

ACKNOWLEDGMENTS

PHOTOGRAPHY BY

Jezz Aliss
Steve Barker
Keith Brenchley
Neil Lawson
Geoff Lee
Warren James Palmer
S.J. Spencer

SPECIAL THANKS TO

Squadron Leader Rick Groombridge
Flight Lieutenant Paul Shenton
Keith Brenchley
Yvonne Walker
All the members of the BBMF
Beckenham Business Systems

Table of Contents

Foreword

Distant memories are hard things to analyse. Which are genuinely remembered? Which are inherited? By that I mean, are some of them memories that were related to you by, say, your parents but so long ago that all you remember is the memory?

Be that as it may, I do remember sitting in our Anderson air raid shelter in the back garden of 27 Salford Road, London SW2 listening to the crump of bombs, doodle-bugs and ack-ack guns and the angry buzz and drone of aircraft as men fought for their very lives above us. I remember the contrails in the sky; the fading drifting proof of the mortal combat that had gone on. Of course, at the age of three I did not know that was what had gone on in the skies over London, but I did inherit the fear and concern of my parents. I do remember sitting on my dad's shoulders in the Mall and Green Park on VE night. It was a brightly coloured, illuminated London, something that I had never seen before, having lived out my whole five and half years in black-out London or the darkened countryside when I was evacuated. I do remember the feeling of happiness and gratitude I sensed in those about me that night.

This is the memory the new generation has inherited from the old. Although they weren't alive then, they have been bequeathed the memory of the gratitude for the courage and sacrifice of the Few and of the Many. This is what the Royal Air Force Battle of Britain Memorial Flight is all about. A flying memorial for all those who in the air and on the ground gave or offered their lives in the air battles of the Second World War. It is also a display team in its own right, on a par with the Red Arrows and just as popular with the new generation as the old.

This book is about the everyday operation and living of 'The Flight' with Warren and Neil everywhere, doing their 'fly on the wall' act. They have captured the ethos and spirit of the BBMF perfectly.

As that little boy who sat on his dad's shoulders on VE night, who, to his own astonishment finds himself 'Boss' of the very team that operates those same aircraft that he heard and watched over fifty years ago, it has been an honour to write this foreword.

Rick Groombridge

Squadron Leader Rick Groombridge
Commanding Officer, BBMF

INTRODUCTION

As a small boy I would lie in bed at night dreaming I was climbing into my Spitfire ready to join the knights in the air. Now as an adult I'm more aware of the huge loss of life that took place on the battlefields in the sky, but my fascination with the combatant aircraft has never diminished. How could such beautiful streamlined machines be so deadly?

If asked, I would have to say that the Spitfire, Hurricane and Lancaster are my favourite objects of desire and I suspect that many people in Britain feel the same. More than any other type, these three aircraft represent the Royal Air Force's 'finest hour' and as the years go by the myth and legend that goes with these classic aircraft continues to fascinate new generations. Generations that have no concept of what 'total warfare' really means. It seems that all those touched by the magic of Merlins are destined to remain under their spell for the rest of their lives.

When I set up Ripping Publishing to publish my favourite sort of books, I realised I finally had the perfect excuse to give vent to my lifetime fascination with these aircraft. What could be more appropriate than to publish a Ripping book on the Spitfire, Hurricane and Lancaster? What better to base the book on than the Royal Air Force Battle of Britain Memorial Flight? Happily the BBMF were as enthused about the idea as I was and went out their way to help Neil and myself with our research. This book is the result of following the BBMF through the fiftieth anniversary year of the end of World War Two.

Once I started working with the BBMF my fascination with the aircraft was matched by a fascination for the people involved with keeping the gems flying. I hope that we manage to pass on to you the reader, a little of the atmosphere and life that goes on behind the scenes, and when you next see the Hurricane, Lancaster and Spitfire at an airshow, you will think about the huge effort that is made to preserve the 'finest hour'.

Special thanks go to the 'Boss', Squadron Leader Rick Groombridge, who allowed me to wander around the flight asking questions of everybody and making a real nuisance of myself. Thanks also to Yvonne and Ted in the office who, I suspect, put up with hell both from pilots and groundcrew and have been so patient in helping with this book. Also special thanks to Flight Lieutenant Paul Shenton who treated Neil and myself as equals. I'm proud to class him as a true friend. Paul believes that the competition glider flying in which Neil and I partake is as dramatic as his Tornado, Spitfire and Hurricane flying. I'm not convinced myself and all I can say is 'Not worthy'! Finally thanks to everyone for all the beers and the good times we enjoyed during the long hot summer of '95.

I hope you enjoy this book and will cheer and support the BBMF in years to come. It would be nice to think that these 'jewels of the sky' are still thrilling crowds well into the 21st century!

Cheers

Warren James Palmer

7

From the Many to the Few

It all started on 15th September 1945 when a Royal Air Force Spitfire and Hurricane flew over a battered but victorious London in the first ever Battle of Britain Flypast. The summer of 1940 when a few pilots and their fighter aircraft held off an aerial armada had already passed into legend. So it was only fitting that on the anniversary of the Battle of Britain's fiercest fighting, there should be a Flypast of the RAF's two main combatant aircraft. So began an annual event to commemorate the Royal Air Force's 'finest hour'.

However, the rapid rate at which Hurricanes and Spitfires were sent to the scrap yard after the war meant that by 1957 there was only one airworthy Hurricane on RAF charge (LF363) and Spitfires were at risk of disappearing completely with the demise of the Meteorological Flight. With wonderful foresight the government of the day, in their haste to reduce these classic aircraft to base metal, had left the RAF without any means of continuing its annual Battle of Britain Flypast. There was a huge outcry both from within the service and from the general public, the result of which was that in June 1957 the civilian pilots of the Meteorological Flight at Woodvale (operated by a division of Short Bros. and Harland) flew three Mk XIX Spitfires back to Duxford. In July 1957, escorted by the latest Hunter and Javelin fighters, the three Spitfires were flown to Biggin Hill where they joined the solitary Hurricane. The Battle of Britain Flight was born, although at that time it was known as the Historic Aircraft Flight.

Unfortunately, the next four years were not kind to the Flight's Spitfires. In September 1957 one Mk XIX (PS915) was removed from the Flight to become a 'gate guardian'. It wasn't until 1984, after British Aerospace decided to spend some tender loving care on PS915 to bring it back to airworthiness, that it was returned to the BBMF. On the bonus side, two Mk XVI Spitfires joined the Flight after being displayed at the 1957 Royal Tournament. Thanks to the instigation of Biggin Hill's station commander, they were restored to flying condition, but only remained at Biggin for a few months. Unfortunately the RAF decided to close Biggin Hill to flying operations, so on 28th February 1958 the two Mk XVIs and one Mk XIX flew to North Weald. They were

Above–The three Spitfires of the civilian-run Meteorological Flight lined up before their attempted return flight to RAF charge at Duxford on 12th June 1957. The Spitfires are PS915, PS853 and PM631.

Above–On the 12th June 1957 the three Spitfires of the THUM Flight made an attempt to return to RAF charge by flying to Duxford in Cambridgeshire. However, PS915 refused to start, PM631 took off but had to return when the radio failed and PS853 took off but turned back with engine trouble. On landing it ran off the runway and nosed over. Not exactly an auspicious start to the Historic Flight! Happily the three aircraft were quickly repaired and PM631 and PS915 flew to Duxford on 14th June, followed by PS853 on the 26th June.

joined a few days later by the solitary Hurricane and other Spitfire Mk XIX which had been delayed at Biggin by a fresh fall of snow. However, the RAF also decided to close North Weald, so on 16th May 1958 the Flight moved yet again, this time to Martlesham Heath. The Flight's stay at North Weald had just been long enough for another Spitfire to be pinched for 'gate guardian' duties. Mk XIX (PS853) went to West Raynham where it was kept in flying condition and finally returned to the Flight in April 1964; the moral here being 'never lend your Spitfire to anyone!'

The annual London Flypast on 20th September 1959 became something of a minor drama when Spitfire Mk XVI SL574 suffered engine failure. The cricket team playing on the Oxo pitch at Bromley in Kent were very surprised when their game was interrupted by a Spitfire force landing on their field. The game later resumed play once the pilot had been shown where to find the telephone in the club house. It hasn't been recorded what the final score was! The MkXVI SL574 never flew with the Historic Flight again and joined the other Mk XVI TE476 (which had been in a landing accident only ten days previously) in early retirement. SL574 is now on display at San Diego, California and TE476 is now flying again with Kermit Week's collection in America.

By the time the Flight moved to Horsham St Faith (now Norwich airport) on 3rd November 1961 it was down to one remaining Mk XIX Spitfire (PM631) and the faithful Hurricane. The next two years were a lean time for the Flight and for some time its very survival was at stake. It wasn't until the next move to Coltishall in April 1963 that the situation gradually improved.

Another outcry both from the public and the service led to one of the original Mk XIXs being returned from 'gate guardian' duties in April 1964 and in that year the three aircraft appeared at a total of fifty air displays across the country. This was heady stuff at the time, but is nothing compared to the 200 displays the BBMF currently appears at each summer. 1965 saw the arrival of a third Spitfire, a Merlin-engined Mk Vb (AB910). Previously owned by Vickers Armstrong, AB910 was flown to Coltishall by Jeffrey Quill, the test pilot responsible for much of the Spitfire's wartime development flying. The Mk Vb was a welcome addition to the Flight especially as it was in many eyes, a 'proper' Spitfire, with the earlier marks' shorter nose, small fin and Merlin engine. In 1968 the film *Battle of Britain* was shot and all the Flight's aircraft were used in the flying sequences, appearing in several different squadron codes. The biggest gain from the film came in the form of Spitfire P7350. The need for more airframes for the film led researchers to look at a Spitfire Mk II in a museum at RAF Colerne. This Spitfire (P7350) was in such good shape, it was decided to restore it to flying condition, and after filming was concluded the Mk II was presented to the Flight. At last the Flight had a Spitfire which actually flew in the Battle of Britain, having served with no 266 Squadron at Hornchurch in 1940!

The future of the Spitfire in the BBMF now seemed assured with a total of four airworthy examples. However, there was still only one airworthy Hurricane (LF363). To guarantee a flying Hurricane at air displays in the future, it was decided to search for another airworthy airframe, a search that led to intervention by the original manufacturers, Hawkers. PZ865 was the last Hurricane ever built by Hawkers and named 'Last of the Many'. Kept by Hawkers as a company aircraft for many years PZ865 was totally refurbished and presented to the Flight in 1972, giving the Flight two airworthy examples of this classic, robust fighter. Although strictly not a Battle of Britain aircraft, Lancaster PA474 was restored to airworthiness by no 44 Squadron who had been the first to be equipped with the type in 1942. PA474 joined the Flight in 1973 when it was decided to rename the Flight as the Battle of Britain Memorial Flight. Today the Lancaster serves as living memorial to all those who lost their lives in the five years of aerial warfare.

The story doesn't quite finish here. Hurricane LF363, the Flight's stalwart machine during the lean years, suffered engine failure in September 1991. The pilot, Squadron Leader Al Martin, searched for somewhere to land dead stick (without power) and headed for RAF Wittering. Unfortunately the aircraft crashed just short of the runway and caught fire, completely gutting the airframe, although happily, the pilot got away with minor injuries. After careful examination of the wreckage it was decided to restore the BBMF's faithful Hurricane

The sad remains of LF363 having being gutted by fire after a forced landing at RAF Wittering on 11th September 1991. Pilot, Squadron Leader Allan Martin suffered engine problems on transit to the Jersey Airshow. He decided to divert to the nearest airfield which was RAF Wittering. As he neared the airfield the Merlin was still running but only just and on approach to the runway the engine cut completely. Finding the path straight ahead blocked Sqn Ldr Martin attempted to turn past the obstacle but LF363's right wingtip touched the ground and the Hurricane cart-wheeled. When LF363 finally came to a rest she was still upright but on fire. Sqn Ldr Martin managed to scrabble clear of the burning wreckage despite a broken ankle. LF363 was completely gutted by the ensuing fire. Later it was discovered that a broken camshaft had jammed the Merlin's inlet valves open, allowing fuel to pour into the hot engine. Happily LF363 is now being restored by Historic Flying Ltd and Sqn Ldr Martin has made a full recovery and is back on BBMF flying duty, albeit with the nickname 'Slam'!

back to airworthy condition. The only problem was a lack of funds. With its usual enthusiasm for supporting vintage aircraft, the government decided not to advance any further funds.

This left the BBMF with no option but to auction one of its Spitfires. PS853 a PR Mk XIX was auctioned in November 1994 and a buyer found—for a short while. The prospective buyer failed to come up with the cash. Euan English, a founding partner of the Squadron club at North Weald, formed a syndicate and 'rescued' the Spitfire, enabling the BBMF to go ahead with its restoration of LF363. On 4th March 1995 Euan English and his son Nicholas were practising formation aerobatics in their Harvard G-TEAC. The Harvard entered a loop but spun out and failed to recover. Euan was killed in the crash and Nicholas suffered serious leg injuries. At time of writing there is a big question mark over the future of the Spitfire PS853 although this tragedy won't affect the restoration of LF363. Being restored by Historic Flying Ltd at Audley End, the BBMF's stalwart Hurricane should take to the air again sometime in late 1996.

Above–15th August 1987 Lancaster PA474 flies past the Blackpool tower. Actually the camera angle makes it look more like the Lanc is about to fly into the tower rather than past it!

Left–This unrepeatable photograph was shot on the 16th August 1960 to mark the 20th anniversary of the Battle of Britain.

From left to right it shows Hurricane LF363 and Spitfire PM631 together with a Meteor 8 of Fighter Command Communications Squadron, a Hunter Mk6 of no74 Squadron, a Javelin Mk9 of no 23 Squadron and a Lightning of the Central Fighter Establishment.

Obviously shot to show the progression of fighters in the RAF, it's slightly ironic that the Spitfire PM631 is the only machine still airworthy. The jet fighters have long since gone to the scrap heap.

Above–An unknown newspaper photograph dated 8th November 1968 announces the Historic Flight's newest recruit. Spitfire Mk II P7350 was a gate guardian at RAF Colerne, near Bath before being put back into the air for the film *Battle of Britain*.

Above–Spitfire PM631 and Hurricane LF363 fly over the South Coast in 1971. Note that the Spitfire pilot is wearing a leather flying helmet in preference to the 'bone domes' that are de rigueur in the Flight today.

Coltishall Hurricane To Keep Flying

The Hawker Hurricane LF363, which left for RAF Coltishall's Battle of Britain Memorial Flight in April bound for the RAF Museum at Hendon, has not come to the end of its flying days after all, it was learned yesterday.

Another Hurricane, a MkI from Bicester, which has seen Battle of France and Battle of Britain service, will go to the museum instead and LF363 will be retained in flying condition.

When LF363 left Coltishall for what looked like its retirement it was replaced by PZ865 the 'Dunsfold' Hurricane presented to the Flight on March 29th by the Hawker Division of Hawker Siddeley. PZ865 'The last of the Many' was the last Hurricane made.

The two Hurricanes flew to RAF Wattisham in April and this was thought to be the last time a pair of this breed of fighter aircraft would be seen flying together. Now, the chances of this happening again have been greatly increased.

Spitfires

The pair will stay with the Flight along with four flying Spitfires. One of the Spits, a MkII, has been using LF363's propeller while its own is being reconditioned.

Both Hurricanes are now at RAF Wattisham and Wing Commander D. Seward of RAF Coltishall, said it was hoped to have the LF363 flying again in two weeks' time. They hoped to have the two machines back at Coltishall by September or October. He said the decision to use the Hurricane from Bicester in the museum was probably due to the fact that it had a more chequered career than LF363. Both LF363 and PZ865 were produced later in the war.

Commenting on the return of LF 363, Wing Commander Seward said, 'We are very pleased. It will give us more flexibility and enable us to have a standby. We think the money spent on maintaining these aircraft is well worthwhile because of the good will they create at air shows.'

Unknown newspaper cutting June 1972

12

Battle 'Spit' crash lands

A Spitfire belonging to Coningsby's famous Battle of Britain Flight crashed in front of 60,000 people on Sunday. Its undercarriage failed as it landed after a display at Duxford Aerodrome in Cambridgeshire.

The pilot, Squadron Leader Geoff Roberts, of Leasingham, escaped unhurt but his aircraft (AB910) lost its four-bladed propeller. However, the Flight is confident of getting the Spitfire, built in 1941, back into the air again.

The accident happened at an air display opened by Battle of Britain fighter hero Sir Douglas Bader.

The Spitfire had landed when there was an undercarriage failure and the aircraft collapsed destroying the four-bladed propeller. This particular mark of Spitfire normally has a three-bladed propeller but, it is understood its own was 'bent' a few weeks ago and the four-bladed wooden one fitted as replacement. It is becoming increasingly difficult to get airscrews for these last remaining machines of the Battle of Britain Memorial Flight, now stationed at RAF Coningsby.

After the crash on Sunday, the remainder of the flying programme was cancelled and the two aircraft still in the air at the time were diverted to Cambridge Airport.

An eyewitness said that fire tenders were quickly on the scene when the Spitfire collapsed. The pilot, he said, appeared dazed and shaken. The Hurricane which was coming in to land behind the Spitfire had to take evasive action and overshoot.

Unknown newspaper cutting, 23rd May 1976

Over the years there have been a number of minor accidents among the BBMF aircraft. The two most serious incidents happening to LF363 and AB910. On 21st August 1978 the Mk V Spitfire AB910 was involved in a taxying accident at an air display at Bex in Switzerland. AB910 was just about to take-off when a Dutch North American Harvard cut across the Spitfires path. The resulting collision caused considerable damage to AB910.

The badly damaged Spitfire was shipped to 5 Maintenance Unit at RAF Kemble in September 1978 where it was discovered that the engine bulkhead, wings, and rear fuselage skinning were badly damaged. Despite this, it was decided to carry out repairs using various components removed from a Spitfire Mk IX which had been stored at RAF St Athan. In January 1980 a second Spitfire, this time a Mk V was used as a three-dimensional model in the final stages of repair. AB910 was returned to the BBMF on 23rd October 1981.

THE LAST SPITFIRE PRANGS

Its duty done, it makes a sudden though not inglorious exit

They said regretfully that the old warrior was really getting past it now, and this must definitely be its last appearance in the London sky. They did not know how right they were when the last Spitfire, Sugar Love 547 soared over Horse Guards Parade yesterday proudly heading the annual Battle of Britain Flypast.

It was 4.30pm. On the saluting base was Mr Harold Macmillan, who had just left the Abbey service of remembrance for the 'Few'.

On the Oxo sports ground outside Bromley the players were walking in for tea. Oxo were 120 for nine in their last match of the season against Old Hollingtonians.

Farewell look

Over Whitehall and Trafalgar Square went the Spitfire and its companion the last Hurricane, and the crowds below looked up in farewell.

Mr Macmillan looked up as well. Down at Bromley, on the Oxo sports ground, assistant groundsman Ray Beavis went out to mark the crease with brush and whitewash bucket. Just after Mr Macmillan had taken his eyes off it, Spitfire Sugar Love was plummeting down slap in the middle of his constituency—and groundsman Ray Beavis was running for his life.

Sugar Love's engine coughed and spluttered as it turned over Crystal Palace. It had had enough, and its pilot, Air Vice Marshal Harold Maguire, DSO, knew it.

Hit Wicket

He looked hurriedly for somewhere to pancake. A sports field. An empty sports field. The field from which Oxo and their opponents has just retired for tea.

Skimming the sightscreen he went in with his flaps down and undercarriage up. He had just 200 yards in which to come to a stop. His wingtip took the ends of the three stumps at one end of the pitch. Crump! Sugar Love hit the grass 60 yards into the outfield. The dust settled over it gently. Its last flight was over.

Groundsman Beavis and a white-coated umpire helped the pilot out and were taken aback to find they had an air vice marshal out there in the deep.

Apology

Pilot Maguire waved to the Hurricane which was circling to see he got down safely, made an explanatory phone call from the pavilion, had tea with the players, and apologised for damaging the wicket.

Then he went to hospital for an X-ray which revealed a strained back and a small bone displaced. Air Vice Marshal Maguire was a Hurricane pilot early in the war. 'No trouble then,' he said ruefully. 'This is my first Battle of Britain injury.'

'It was tough having to end up this way. The engine cut out almost entirely. At least it was a good landing.'

14

Play Resumes

Then he flew back from Biggin Hill to his base at Martesham, Suffolk, where the RAF's one other Spitfire is out to grass.

Sugar Love was pushed over the boundary, the propeller, undercarriage, and one wing broken. Its last Battle of Britain mission was over. So was the tea interval on the Bromley ground.

One tradition may have been broken, but in accordance with another older tradition play was resumed between Oxo and Old Hollingtonians.

Round the boundary now were three fire engines, some police cars, and several hundred spectators whom the cricket had failed to attract.

The wicket, thanks to the impact of Sugar Love's last landing, was taking a spin.

Daily Express, Monday 21st September 1959

An air vice marshal with some explaining to do makes a call from the Oxo pavilion.

SUPERMARINE SPITFIRE MK XIX. THE LAST OPERATIONAL SPITFIRE STILL FLYING AT R.A.F. BIGGIN HILL. SEPT 1957.

PM631 was one of the original two Mk XIX Spitfires flown to Biggin Hill on 14th July 1957 to form the Historic Aircraft Flight, which later became known as the BBMF. At one stage in 1961 she was the Flight's only Spitfire and soldiered on through the difficult years with her stablemate Hurricane LF363. Built after the war in November 1945, PM631 spent most of her time in storage before being allotted to the Meteorological Flight in April 1952. This photograph of PM631 was taken at Biggin Hill in September 1957.

15

Above–This undated photograph shows Lancaster PA474 flying over a squadron of Vulcans, probably belonging to 44 Squadron based at RAF Waddington, where PA474 was originally restored. The lack of mid-upper turret dates the photograph as sometime before 1976, the year the turret was fitted to PA474.

Above–'What beautiful lines and the aircraft ain't bad either!' is the caption on this 1970 photograph of Flight Lieutenant Bill Moxon and an unknown young beauty queen. Sometimes BBMF life can be hell.

Spitfire show sparks low flying fury

A SPITFIRE air display over Newton Aycliffe has prompted a call for controls on low flying.

Several people living in the Horndale area of the town were alarmed to see the lone Spitfire flying beneath the clouds during a special display routine for the Great Aycliffe show.

Anxious neighbours contacted ward Councillor Tony Moore who has called for a review of local by-laws which enabled the plane to fly so low over the town.

The display was one of the main attractions of the Great Aycliffe show with staff from the Battle of Britain Memorial Flight invited to the North-East to stage the demonstration.

Roger Braney, at the Teesside airport air traffic control tower, said the bad weather had affected the display which the Spitfire crew had hoped to carry out.

Mr Braney said: "Obviously the Spitfire had to fly low to be visible below the clouds but I cannot believe the Flight was a danger."

Councillor Moore telephoned the Newton Aycliffe police but Sgt Stephen Bell said the Flight had been agreed and arranged through all the appropriate authorities and the police had not dealt with any other complaints from the public.

But Councillor Moore said he is concerned by the possible risks posed by low flying aircraft over built-up areas.

"If that plane had crashed the consequences do not bear thinking about," he said.

High winds and continuous rain yesterday sparked an early morning drama at the show.

The stormy weather brought down a marquee containing more than 800 craft exhibits at about 7.45am. Show organisers and members of the northern Vintage Transport Association rallied round to save the produce, which had been judged on Saturday.

The Northern Echo, Monday, 31st August, 1992

You can't please all the people all the time!

16

Should the Lanc be pensioned off?

THE crash at the Biggin Hill Battle of Britain air display of a wartime bomber must raise the query — is it safe for these old aircraft to take to the air?

We in Lincolnshire have a particular interest in this, some people having fought so hard and for so long to ensure that the last Lancaster bomber in flying condition is kept within the county boundaries. It takes to the air fairly frequently — it was busy showing itself off, with a Spitfire and a Hurricane, during the weekend's Battle of Britain commemoration — and there can be no question about the care that is taken of it.

The people at Coningsby RAF station who are responsible for its maintenance must love it dearly — but the fact remains that such things grow old and, however meticulous the routine examinations to which it is subject a little fault can arise in some out-of-the-way corner.

A tiny bolt may develop a hairline crack that escapes detection. And from that it is easy to imagine a rapid spread of damage. The Lancaster is 35 years old and, nostalgic though it is to hear it roaring overhead we in Lincolnshire can never forget the sound of those engines — is it not time it was mothballed?

There is an ideal "old aircrafts' home" for it, down in Bedfordshire which itself has local connections. The Shuttleworth Collection of historic aircraft at Old Warden, near Biggleswade was founded on money left by Lincoln industrialist Alfred Shuttleworth nearly 60 years ago.

He died a millionaire and a considerable slice of his cash went to a favourite nephew, Richard Ormonde Shuttleworth, who was then able to fulfil an ambition — to set up an aircraft museum. He was killed in a flying accident during the war but his mother, Mrs Frank Shuttleworth, founded the memorial trust which enabled his name and interests to be perpetuated.

In the collection are aircraft going back to Bleriot's time, through those in service in the two world wars. "Our" Lancaster would feel very much at home there — and would then never face the possible hazard that marred the Biggin Hill event.

Chronicle, 2nd October 1980

Happily nobody paid much attention to this article. However, the lack of knowledge exhibited by the media and public can be alarming. It's a shame this journalist didn't talk to the engineers at the BBMF first. Maybe they could have put his mind at rest by informing him that he was far more likely to win the pools than be hit by bits of a Lancaster!

Right–This 1973 photograph shows the full complement of Spitfires and Hurricanes flying over the Channel.

The Mk V Spit AB910 is in the foreground followed by Mk II P7350. The two Hurricanes PZ865 and LF363 are next followed by the later mark Spitfires PM631 and PS853.

17

KEEPING MEMORIES ALIVE

Each year millions of people flock to air displays throughout the country and although for many people the stars of the show are the supersonic fighters and the aerobatic teams, to the older generation it is the sight of the Spitfire and Hurricane which stays in the mind.

The vintage Second World War fighters come from the Battle of Britain Memorial Flight, which is based at Coltishall, some ten miles, north-east of Norwich.

The Flight, commanded during the 1973 season by Sqn Ldr Bill Gambold, consists of four Spitfires— ranging from a IIa which flew from Hornchurch during the Battle of Britain to the PR19 built in 1945—and two Hurricane IIC fighters dating from 1944.

It was formed at Biggin Hill in 1957 and was based at Martlesham Heath and Horsham St Faith before moving to its present base in 1964.

The six aircraft are flown by RAF pilots based at Coltishall. When there is a vacancy in the Flight volunteers are sought on the station. There are always many people anxious to have the opportunity of flying such thoroughbred fighters, and the choice, made by the station commander and the CO of the operations wing, takes into account previous piston-engined and display experience. Normally the pilots are serving ground tours on the station.

The aim, as Flt Lt Pete Gostick, the training officer with the Battle of Britain Memorial Flight, says is "to show off the aeroplane rather than the skills of the pilot". With aerobatic teams the reverse is true.

The Flight has its own Chipmunk, and once he has been selected the new pilot flies this, with a QFI (Qualified Flying Instructor), to acquire the feel of a piston-engined aircraft with a tail wheel.

Harvard

The new pilot's next stage is to visit the RAE at Boscombe Down, where he flies dual in a Harvard two-seat trainer. Then he has his first flight. After a thorough briefing on the aircraft's handling, checks, speeds, power settings and everything else he needs to know, the pilot takes off in one of the Hurricanes.Throughout his sortie he is watched from the Coltishall control tower by the OC (Officer Commanding) of the operations wing, Wg Cdr D.J. Seward, and the training officer.

After up to six flights in a Hurricane the new pilot goes through the same procedure in one of the earlier Merlin-engined Spitfires. Then he is considered qualified to give displays in either type. After the pilot has gained experience on the Hurricanes and early Spitfires he converts to the more powerful Spitfire PR19s, which are powered by Griffon engines.

During 1973 the Battle of Britain Flight gave about eighty displays, some with a single aircraft, others with two of the fighters giving a synchronised display.

When a Hurricane and Spitfire appear together there is a set routine, but when one aircraft is giving a solo performance the pilot decides on his own show, depending on the frontage of the crowd.

Limitations

Even the later Spitfires are now nearly thirty years old and strict limitations have been placed on their flying, which does not exceed a combined total of 200 hours flying for the six aircraft.

At no time is the speed permitted to exceed 275 knots and, apart from a take-off and landing, there is a minimum height of 100ft. A stress limit of 3G has been placed on the aircraft, which means that no aerobatics can be performed. This limits the displays to steep turns and wing-overs.

The members of the Flight are very conscious of the rarity of the aircraft. "They are national treasures," says Sqn Ldr A.L. Veasey, the senior engineering officer with responsibility for the Flight, "and everybody treats them as such".

Celebrations

It is hoped to ensure that at least one Spitfire and Hurricane will be able to take part in the fiftieth anniversary celebrations of the Battle of Britain in 1990.

This means that great efforts are made to ensure the reliability of the aircraft. Sqn Ldr Veasey emphasises that the same servicing standards and policies are employed in the Memorial Flight as in any other RAF unit.

Chf Tech Dick Melton tries to obtain spares for one of the aircraft from one of his 'sources'.

But although the six veteran fighters are Coltishall responsibility, many other stations are involved in their well-being. All the resurfacing and painting work is done at Kemble, while Bicester weighs the aircraft and determines their centre of gravity.

Third line servicing of the radio is carried out at Sealand, the cartridge starters used in the Griffon engines of the Spitfire PR19s are serviced at Mount Batten, and St Athan manufactures components that cannot be obtained. Also, Strike Command has officers designated as the engineering authorities for the aircraft.

Liaison

Help comes from outside the RAF as well. One of the Hurricanes was given by Hawker Siddley, with whom a close liaison is maintained. The engines go to Rolls-Royce for overhaul and Dunlops make tyres and inner tubes from the original moulds. Help is given to, and received from, Strathallan Air Services, where Sir William Roberts has the only other flying Hurricane in Britain.

Spares are a problem, and aviation enthusiasts are sometimes able to give the Flight small items which are hard to find elsewhere.

Parts sought

Even now there are items which the Flight is seeking. Propellers are not easy to obtain, and smaller parts such as brake valves and exhaust stubs, are also difficult to find.

But in the end maintenance comes down to the skill of the small team of eleven groundcrew from all trades whose full-time task is the servicing of the six fighters. Each time the aircraft go to give a display, three of the crew fly in a 207 Squadron Basset which accompanies the fighters. And next year the groundcrew will be even more involved, as the Lancaster bomber has been recently moved to Coltishall from Waddington.

The groundcrew, says Sqn Ldr Veasey, must have enthusiasm. And it helps if they have experience on the older propeller-driven aircraft.

At work on a Merlin engine on the bench (left) are Cpl Steve Langton and Chf Tech Sandy Lerski. For major overhauls the engines are sent to Rolls -Royce.

Maintenance

So high is the standard of maintenance achieved by the Battle of Britain groundcrew, led by Chief Technician Dick Melton, that of the ninety-six shows planned for the 1973 season, eighty were flown and sixteen cancelled for weather reasons.

The one remaining show that was cancelled was the fourth display scheduled for one of the Spitfires on the RAF's At Home Day in September to mark the Battle of Britain.

The vintage aircraft are very popular with the pilots on the Battle of Britain Flight.

Easy to Fly

Flight Lieutenant Pete Gostick says that both the Spitfires and the Hurricanes seem to have been designed as simple aircraft to fly, so that the pilot was able to concentrate on fighting.

"If you can fly one of today's light aircraft," he says, " you can fly a Spitfire. Compared with even the Hunter the work load is negligible."

Many thousands of RAF and civil pilots would like the opportunity of flying a Spitfire, but are never likely to get the chance. The fortunate few that do fly one of these Second World War veterans look upon it as one of the highlights of their RAF careers. And who can blame them?

Written by Michael Hill, RAF News, 5th January 1974

A good day's flying and a glorious sunset — life doesn't get much better than this!

Sunset on an airfield somewhere in England. Actually the airfield is Biggin Hill and the sunset is in France. Ask any pilot and he will tell you there's something magic about airfields when the sun goes down — especially when the aircraft involved are a Spitfire and Lancaster!

Above–Hurricane PZ865 tucks up close to the Lancaster as they fly around the coastline of Jersey en-route for the annual Battle of Britain air display. When flying long distances the Lancaster acts as a 'shepherd' for the fighters which do not have any navigational aids.

Above–Hurricane PZ865 and the Mk Vb Spitfire AB910 tuck up in line astern formation behind the rear turret of the Lancaster. The rear turret has a clear view panel through which it is possible to take stunning photographs like this.

Above–The Mk II Spit P7530 and the MK Vb AB910 line up beside the Lancaster for this shot taken from the BBMF's Dakota.

Above–Lining up a four-engined bomber for a flypast takes some practice! Arriving at the right spot at the right time takes precise flying and navigation. The BBMF crews did a magnificent job flying over London for the VE and VJ celebrations where split-second timing was essential.

Spitfire Mk IIA P7350

P7530 is in fact the only aircraft in the Battle of Britain Memorial Flight that actually flew in the air battles of 1940. She is also the world's oldest airworthy Spitfire having been built as a Mk IIA at the Castle Bromwich aircraft factory, one of a production run of 750 units built after June 1940. To the purist's eye, P7530 is arguably the definitive Battle of Britain Spitfire, presenting itself with extremely clean, uncluttered lines without the longer nose and larger fin of the Griffon-powered Spitfires. Within the Flight she is known as a 'baby' Spit being lighter and less powerful than the Mk XIXs.

Our research shows that she flew with no 64 Squadron (sqn code-SH) just at the end of the Battle of Britain in October 1940. Indeed not only did P7530 fly in the battle, she was actually shot down! At ten past ten on the morning of Friday 25th October 1940, Pilot Officer B. Martel of no 603 Squadron 11 Group, Hornchurch, engaged an unspecified number of Messerchmitt Bf 109s over Hastings in Kent. Unfortunately both he and P7350 came out the worse for the encounter. Where he made his forced landing we don't know, but within a short time P7530 was repaired and back on squadron service. A close look at the top wing surfaces reveals small metal inserts which were standard bullet damage repair during the Battle of Britain. These would seem to be physical proof of P7350's encounter with the Bf 109s on that fateful Friday. However, P7350 exacted her revenge in the period up to 1942 being responsible for three aerial victories.

As with so many of the Spitfires of that period, P7530 never stayed with one squadron for too long. Combat aircraft were moved around to wherever they were needed and P7530 was no exception. She later saw combat further north in the country in 'Sector K', with 266 Rhodesia Squadron of 12 Group at Wittering. P7530 was then transferred to no 616 South Yorkshire Sqn at Kirton-in-Lindsey, then the Central Gunnery School, no 57 Operational Training Unit, and finally no 39 Maintenance Unit. After such a long period of active service P7530 was finally, at the end of the war, discharged from RAF service, albeit very briefly. Private buyer, John Dale Ltd purchased P7530 and re-presented the aircraft to the aircraft museum at RAF Colerne. There she remained the pride of the collection until 1967 when the producers of a new film called *The Battle of Britain* were searching for suitable airframes for use as 'extras'. On close examination of P7530 it was decided that she could be restored to flying condition. Given the civil registration G-AWIJ, she played a starring role as the only genuine airworthy 1940 veteran. On completion of filming she was presented back to the RAF where she has been kept in airworthy condition ever since.

For the 1995 flying season she wore the markings of P7832 RN-S of no 72 Basutoland Squadron bearing the name *Enniskillen* which is representative of one of the 'presentation' Spitfires. These aircraft were given the names of their sponsor or fund raiser who had raised the cost of a new aircraft through the Spitfire fund. In the case of the *Enniskillen* the cash came from the Belfast *Telegraph* newspaper who also raised funds for seven other Spitfires.

Battle Spit Gift to Coltishall

A Spitfire which took part in the Battle of Britain, was yesterday undergoing acceptance tests as the newest recruit at RAF Coltishall's Historic Flight.

The aircraft—P7350—was presented to Coltishall, home of the Battle of Britain Memorial Flight, by the makers of the film about the Battle, now in preparation, in return for the help the RAF gave them during the exterior shooting this summer.

Its arrival at Coltishall brings the Historic Flight strength to five—one Mk II Spitfire, one Mk V, two Mk 19s and a Mk II Hurricane— but it is the only one

actually to have fought in the battle, flying with 266 Squadron in September 1940.

The film company, Spitfire Productions, found the plane at RAF Colerne near Bath, where it adorned the station gatepost, and put it into flying condition.

It was flown to Coltishall by Sqn Ldr Tim Mills from Cranwell, and received for the station by Wng Cdr. George Black, O/C Flying.

Newspaper cutting, 8th November 1968

29

Above–Before starting, the Merlin engines have to be primed. This is done from the cockpit using a small hand-operated pump. Over priming can cause excess fuel to burn off with a dramatic flash of flame that exits from the exhaust stubs.

The BBMF enjoys a close relationship with some of the original manufacturers such as Rolls-Royce, Dowty-Rotol and Supermarine who of course became part of British Aerospace. Although the stocks of original parts have long since disappeared these companies have been instrumental in manufacturing new spares to keep the BBMF fleet flying. British Aerospace fashioned a replacement radiator for Spitfire Mk V AB910 in the mid-seventies. Dunlop tyres have also proved to be a great help to the Flight. In the early seventies the Mk XIXs had to fly with Buccaneer nose wheel tyres until Dunlop produced a batch of replacement tyres. They also produced replacement rubber bags for the pneumatic brakes and more recently they produced a batch of huge mainwheel tyres for the Lancaster.

Below–When not flying the aircraft of the BBMF have their engines run up once a week.

Above–For many P7350 is the most 'authentic' of the BBMF Spitfires. In terms of appearance it is markedly different from the later Mk XIXs. The nose is much shorter, being powered by a single stage supercharged Merlin compared to the much bigger Griffon engine of the later marks. The fin is R.J. Mitchell's original design rather than the larger tail unit needed on the later Spits to deal with the increased torque of the more powerful engines. The Mk II also has a three-blade propeller rather than the five blade of the Mk XIXs. Once again the later marks needed extra bladed propellers to absorb the huge amounts of extra power. The Merlin III which powered the Mk I Spitfires during the Battle of Britain had an output of 1,050HP while the Griffon 61 of the Mk 22 Spitfire had an incredible output of over 2,000HP.

Spitfire Mk Vb AB910

One of a total of 3,003 Mk Vbs produced, AB910 rolled off the Castle Bromwich production line one year after the Flight's Mk II P7530, in August 1941. Like most Spitfires at that time, AB910 moved from squadron to squadron as the need arose. She served with no 222 (Natal) Squadron, no 130 (Punjab) Squadron, no 133 (Eagle) Squadron, no 242 (Canadian) Squadron, no416 (RCAF) Squadron, no 407 (RCAF) Squadron and no 527 Squadron, plus several maintenance units.

However, she slipped into aviation folklore in 1945 whilst with no 53 Operational Training Unit at Hibaldstow. It was customary during the war for groundcrew to provide the necessary ballast during ground engine runs to stop the tailplane from rising and so causing the prop to chew up the ground. This was done by simply lying across one side of the tailplane. On one bright and breezy day the pilot, Flight Lieutenant Neil Cox completed his ground runs as usual and took off. Unfortunately he failed to notice that Leading Aircraft Woman Margaret Horton was still admirably performing her duties as a tail anchor and was desperately clinging on for dear life to the tailplane. He completed a circuit of the airfield and touched down safely wondering why AB910 was so tail heavy. When AB910 finally came to a halt, he climbed out of the cockpit and was somewhat surprised to find Margaret still hanging on to the tailplane shaken but otherwise none the worse for her unauthorised joy ride! Leading Aircraft Woman Horton became the only known person to have flown 'on' rather than 'in' a Spitfire!

Like the BBMF's other 'baby' Spit, AB910 was de-mobbed and went into civvy street in 1947 under the guise G-AISV. Unfortunately, while competing in the 1953 King's Cup Air Race, a heavy landing resulted in her having to be rebuilt by Vickers. Twelve years later after much love, care and attention, AB910 reappeared bearing her original serial number plus the squadron code QJ-J. The Supermarine test pilot, Jeffrey Quill, flew AB910 to Cottishall to join the Historic Aircraft Flight.

AB910 has had her fair share of 'incidents' since joining the BBMF. In October 1972 she suffered an undercarriage failure at RAF Coltishall which resulted in repairs being made to the right wing. In June 1976 she tipped up onto her nose at an airshow at Duxford, and at Bex in Switzerland she was involved in a taxying collision with a Harvard. This resulted in major repairs being carried out and parts being donated from a Mk IX Spitfire in RAF storage.

For the 1995 season AB910 carried the distinctive and classic invasion stripes from 6th June 1944 when she wore the codes letters AE-H of no 402 Squadron supporting the Normandy invasion.

Above–Miss Becky Sharpe preparing for the 1950 King's Cup Air Race in which she flew AB910.

Of the 22,742 Spitfires and Seafires built, only a few remain in flying condition in Britain with a few more in various parts of the world. AB910, owned by British Aircraft Corporation, is the oldest example of a Spitfire in flying condition anywhere. It is flown today by David Morgan who flew Seafires with the Fleet Air Arm and has been a test pilot with the company since 1950.

This modified Spitfire Mk Vb was originally delivered to no 92 Squadron of the RAF in 1942 from Vickers' Castle Bromwich factory. The squadron letters it bears today, QJ-J, were in fact used by no92 for one of their Spitfires at that time. After the war this aircraft was bought by Air Commodore A.H. Wheeler, CBE and eventually came into the possession of Vickers. On examination, it was found that its condition needed a complete dismantling and rebuilding exercise which was carried out almost as a solo job by Arthur Luscombe, Supermarine's ground engineer at South Marston Works, and checked by L.D. Ashby, the approved works inspector there. It is now based at the BAC flight test airfield at Wisley, near the company's Weybridge Works.

This rebuilding necessitated the acquisition or fabrication of many spare parts and this has proved harder and harder in practice as remaining examples of Spitfires disappear like magic on the scrap merchant's heap. In this work, much assistance has been rendered by the original suppliers of accessories and materials. The windscreen was taken off a scrap heap as was the rear view mirror from an old motor car dump.

When the aeroplane was taken over by Vickers, it was fitted with a Rolls-Royce Merlin 55M engine, which powered the Seafire Mk II naval version of the Spitfire. This engine has a good low-level performance and was rebuilt by Rolls-Royce and is maintained by their service engineers. The propeller was taken from a Mk IX Spitfire and was rebuilt in 1962 by Rotol.

Printed by the British Aircraft Corporation in 1963

Right–AB910 sits on the Tarmac at an airshow in 1965. In the background can be seen PZ865 which at that time was owned and operated by Hawkers just as AB910 was operated by Supermarine. The display pilot was Jefferey Quill.

A NEAR MISS!

How ACW2 Horton logged ten minutes flying time. **November 1948**

A SAILOR would say it all came of setting off on a Friday. Some people blamed me for not telling the conductor to put me off at the penny stage. Anyone who had worked on any Flight at RAF station Hibaldstow in February, 1945, would tell you it was no more than could be expected of *T-for-Trouble*.

She bad been my charge for months before she presented her best trick, but that doesn't mean she had given us a dull time. Hardly a day passed without the mechanics, making tracks for the crew-room after thankfully seeing the last kite of the detail take off, being arrested by the unwelcome sight of one lone Spitfire returning to the dispersal. 'That'll be *T-for-Trouble*!' I used to groan to the fitter, and *T-for-Trouble* it almost invariably was. She reminded me of one of those wicked old horses that delight in putting their rider unexpectedly into the ditch but stop at breaking his neck. 'She's always in mischief but she always brings 'em back alive!' I said reassuringly one day to a pilot who had heard of the old kite's jinx, little realising how strikingly I was to illustrate my own statement.

At Hibaldstow the order 'Rough Weather Procedure' received from Air Traffic Control meant that every taxying Spitfire must have a mechanic sitting on its tail unit before it reached the runway, to prevent the aircraft being blown on to its nose. On this particular day the order was shouted to me by one of the sergeants as I hurried down to the bay where *T-for-Trouble* was just being started up, so calling out to a corporal who was pulling away the trolley-acc that I would take his place on the tailplane, I jumped up on the starboard side and settled myself comfortably with the fin behind my back.

We had reached the runway intersecting the one actually in use, and I was waiting for the aircraft to slow up for me to slip down, when I suddenly realised that she was increasing speed. It was too late to jump off, so I flung myself across the fuselage and grasped the elevator on the port side in a vain effort to attract the pilot's attention. Even before I had given up the attempt the change of movement told me that we were actually "upstairs." There was nothing to hold on to but the cut-away corner of the elevator into which I had inserted three fingers, but I had no sensation of slipping. The fin prevented my rolling forwards over the

Right – Margaret Horton shows how she clung to 'T-for-Trouble'

38

tail, and the force of the slipstream gave a feeling of solidity to the air. Meanwhile the pilot, his elevator almost u/s was having a bad time. Having laboured round the circuit, still unaware of the cause of his trouble, he wirelessed for permission to land. At the same moment the telephone message from the Flight telling of my predicament reached the officer in the control tower, who ordered the pilot to land forthwith, without warning him that the cause of his trouble was a 9-stone gremlin.

The wisdom of this decision was proved by the pilot's perfect landing, so gentle that even after feeling the aircraft suddenly drop a few feet I did not realise the cause until a resumption of the sensation of speed, of which one is unconscious in the air, announced that we were back on the runway. *T-for-Trouble* came back none the worse for her little joke, and is now probably enjoying a hearty whinny over the story along with Pegasus and Stephenson's Rocket in whatever celestial stable immortal steeds are accommodated. My 'AB910' was posted from the station soon after this prank, and the only keepsake I have of the Battle-of-Britain veteran is a scrap of Perspex from the hood which she tossed off in the air in one of her caprices.

My friends said I must have been dozing on duty, and if I had fallen off at 600 feet it would have taught me a lesson, to which my answer is that it only proves that *you can't keep a good WAAF down*.

Others asked why the 'Rough Weather' order to warn the pilot that his aircraft had a passenger failed to reach him before he set off; why the airfield controller didn't see me before he gave permission for the take-off, and why the ambulance had not even left sick quarters by the time I had walked back to the crewroom, instead of being ready by the runway in case I was flung off when we landed. I am still wondering why I didn't notice the green light in time to fling myself off, even at the risk of a broken limb. I can't answer these questions, but they all seem to point to the same moral—that dealing with modern aircraft isn't the same as dozing behind a country dobbin, and whether you're air or ground crew, every moment you're on duty you must be, in both senses of the phrase, 'on the spot'.

Article written for the 'Aeroplane' magazine in November 1948

Above–Another shot of AB910 shortly after her landing accident at Duxford in 1976. Still getting into trouble all these years after Margaret Horten's escapade, AB910 has had more than her fair share of 'incidents'.

Above–AB910 displaying her classic Spitfire lines. For many AB910 and P7350 are the epitome of R.J. Mitchell's design, being Merlin rather than Griffon powered. The baby Spits also have shorter noses and original fin shape of the early marks of Spitfire.

Left and opposite–Two views of the cockpit of AB910. As with all the BBMF's aircraft, AB910 is kept as authentic as possible. However, it is not always possible to fit or use original parts. Sometimes compromises have to be made in the interests of safety.

As an example, all the BBMF's aircraft have been rewired. During the war electrical systems were all 12 volts, however modern aircraft now use a 24-28 volt system. As it was becoming increasingly difficult to find 12v rated components the decision was made to upgrade the electrics.

Modern radios are also carried in all the aircraft, rather than the original valve sets. Such was the weight of these original sets that extra ballast has to be fitted in the tail to compensate for the lighter modern radio gear. However, none of the fighters are fitted with modern navigation aids, so on long trips they have to be 'shepherded' either by the Lancaster or Dakota. One wonders how long it will be before the temptation of carrying small hand-held GPS (Global Positioning System) becomes too much!

Guns and ammunition have also been stripped from the fighters. The cannon muzzles on AB910 are mock-ups rather than the genuine article.

Spitfire Mk XIX PM631

PM631 is the youngest in terms of date of construction of the BBMF Spitfires. She was delivered to the RAF in November 1945 and took up duties with no 203 Advanced Flying School in May 1949. The following year she was leant to Short Brothers and engaged in Temperature and Humidity Monitoring whilst based at Horton Park in Woodvale. PM631 might be the youngest of the Spits but at thirty eight years on RAF charge, she is the longest serving of all the Spits being one of the original aircraft to join the Historic Aircraft Flight at Biggin Hill on 14th July 1957 after transfer from the 'THUM' Flight.

She is not a pure fighter, having been built and operated as a photo reconnaissance aircraft. A close inspection will reveal many differences both internally and externally between the 'baby' Spits and the PRXIX. Instead of the Merlin, she is powered by a Rolls-Royce Griffon 66 engine with a five-blade propeller to absorb all that extra power. This gives PM631 a top speed of 446mph compared to the 370mph of the Mk II Spitfire.

By removing the guns and ammunition from the wings, it was possible to carry more fuel giving the PRXIX a much greater range of 1,550 miles compared to the 395 miles of the earlier Mk II Spitfire. However, the extra power of the Griffon can lead to handling problems for the pilots. The torque of the mighty Griffon tends to swing PM631 to the right on take-off, while the Merlin-engined Mk II and Mk V tend to swing the other way, to the left. PM631 also has a much longer, heavier nose than the Merlin-engined Spitfires, and this can make taxying a problem. It's widely recognised amongst the BBMF pilots that the Mk XIX Spitfires can 'bite' far more than the 'baby' Spitfires, and consequently they are the last machines an up-and-coming BBMF pilot will convert to.

In 1964 PM631 together with PS853 spent some time with the Air Development Squadron at RAF Binbrook. There the venerable Mk XIX Spitfires were flown against the latest Javelin and Lightning interceptors in mock

46

combat. This was at the time of troubles in Indonesia and the RAF needed to know how effective Lightnings and Javelins would be against the older generation of piston-engined fighters still operated in that part of the world. It was discovered that as long as the jets kept fast and could get in behind unseen (which is the only place an infra-red missile could acquire a decent heat source) and effectively made slashing attacks, the Spits would be unable to bring their guns to bear. There is a rumour that the simulator at Coningsby has, in the past, been set to fly a Sidewinder armed Spitfire against the latest F3 Tornado. The result apparently was a number of wins for the Spitfire!

For the 1995 airshow season, PM631 wore the colour scheme of a no 11 Squadron Mk XIV based in south-east Asia.

Above–September 1957 and PM631 is the last Spitfire still flying on RAF charge. This photograph was taken at Biggin Hill a few months after PM631 was transferred from the Meteorological Flight.

Below–PM631 in formation with the other original member of the Historic Aircraft Fight, Hurricane LF363. The pair are seen here on the way to an airshow at Boscombe Down in 1971.

47

Spitfire Mk XIX PS915

PS915 was one of the last batch of seventy nine PR XIXs delivered to the RAF from November 1944 onwards. PS915 however, missed the war in Europe by a matter of days being delivered to no 541 Squadron at RAF Benson some time in June 1945. Like PM631 she is an unarmed camera ship and as such was moved to the RAF's PR development unit and used as a test bed for research into photo-reconnaissance.

Her next move was to Windslof in Germany where with the squadron code OI-K she was used to fly long-range PR missions. These missions took place over what was later to become known as the 'Iron Curtain'.

After a spell at no 9 Maintenance Unit at Cosford in 1951, she joined PM631 and the Meteorological Flight at Woodvale. In 1957 she joined the other Spitfires at Biggin Hill forming the original Historic Flight, but it wasn't long before PS915 was 'borrowed' to become a gate guardian first at West Malling, then Leuchars and Brawdy. In fact PS915 spent more than thirty years as a gate guardian. In 1977 the BBMF looked at replacing the Griffon 66 engines in the Mk XIX Spitfires with Griffon 58 engines from Avro Shakletons. By machining the rear casing of the supercharger and removing some unwanted support lugs a Griffon Mk 58 was finally fitted to PS915, the evaluation being carried out by Rolls-Royce at East Kilbride in Scotland. The work itself was carried out by the BBMF and RAF St Athan. British Aerospace then undertook a full restoration of the airframe and after a very long absence PS915 finally rejoined the BBMF in 1987.

For the 1995 season PS915 wore the colours of the prototype Mk XIV JF319. This was in recognition of the sterling work carried out by the wartime test pilots at Boscombe Down and Supermarine Aviation.

Right–Corporal Fiona Holding helps Squadron Leader Paul Day strap into the cockpit of PS915 prior to another display in August 1995.

Above–The later marks of Spitfire have greater range than the 'baby' Spits so tend to be aircraft allocated by the Flight for displays that entail long ferry distances. The longer noses of the Griffon-engined Spitfires require careful handling on the ground. It's necessary for the pilot to swing the nose from side to side during taxying to enable him to see ahead as there is no view over the nose when the tail is on the ground.

Below– After the display PS915 is refuelled. PS915 has fuel tanks both in the wings and in the fuselage. The Mk XIX Sptifires particularly were chosen for meteorological work during the 1950s as their large internal fuel tanks gave a duration of over four hours whilst the pressurised cockpit allowed operation at high altitudes without too much pilot fatigue.

Hurricane Mk IIc PZ865

The Hurricane's role in the Battle of Britain has always been overshadowed by that of the Spitfire. Even though there were more Hurricanes in the battle it probably comes down to aesthetics as to why the Spitfire became so much more popular in the public's imagination. The classic clean lines and elliptical wing represent for many people the epitome of what a wartime fighter should look like, but it should always be remembered that during the battle it was the lesser Hurricane which scored the majority of the kills.

PZ865 did not, unfortunately, see action in the Battle of Britain. In fact she was the 14,533rd Hurricane built and the very last. Named the 'Last of the Many' she left Hawker's production line on 27th June 1944. She was rolled out together with Hawker's sole remaining Hart covered in a banner proclaiming the many areas of conflict the Hurricane fighter flew in. The first test flight was made by George Bulman who had also flown the prototype Hurricane on her first flight back in November 1935.

However, it wasn't until March 1972 that PZ865 was brought onto RAF charge. Up until then PZ865 was used as a communications and test machine for Hawker's. Like the Mk V Spitfire AB910 she spent some time in the fifties as a racing machine and achieved a creditable second place in the 1950 King's Cup Race. At this time she carried the civilian registration G-AMAU on a fetching royal blue with gold colour scheme, a scheme most appropriate to her sponsor, HRH the Princess Margaret. The pilot for much of the flying in the King's Cup was a certain Group Captain Peter Townsend.

Back in wartime markings PZ865 appeared in the films *Angels One Five* and *Reach for the Sky* in the late fifties. PZ865 found itself a new job in the early sixties during the development of the Hawker-Siddley P1127 Kestrel, the forerunner of the famous Harrier. The low-speed handling made her ideal as a chase plane for the prototype 'jump-jet' particularly in the transition trials from vertical to normal flight. Once again PZ865 became a film star in 1968 when she was one of the flying 'stars' in the film *Battle of Britain*. After completion of filming she remained on static display at the Hawker museum until she was once more restored to flying condition in 1971 and presented to the BBMF at RAF Coltishall on 30th March 1972.

For the 1995 season PZ865 wore the Mediterranean camouflage of a no 261 Squadron Hurricane. Representative of an 'Operation Hurry' machine, one of the twelve Hurricanes onboard the aircraft carrier HMS *Argus* bound for Malta and as such PZ865 salutes those personnel serving with the Mediterranean Air Force during WWII.

Above–June 1944 and PZ865 the 14,533rd and last Hurricane to be built is rolled out. The banner hung over the cockpit recalls the many areas of conflict the Hurricane flew in. Throughout her production a banner declaring PZ865 as the 'Last of the Many' was hung over the airframe and later written on the side of the fuselage just below the cockpit. Despite being replaced by the Typhoon and Tempest in the frontline in the European conflict, the Hurricane continued to serve in the frontline in several battle zones right up to the end of the war, particularly in south-east Asia.

Below–PZ865 carries out her flight test in the summer skies of England in 1944. Although she's carrying the standard Mk II armament of four cannons, PZ865 never fired her guns in anger. In fact she never saw wartime RAF service, being bought back from the Air Ministry by Hawkers and used as a test and communications machine. At the controls is George Bulman who flew the prototype Hurricane from Brooklands in November 1935.

57

Above–PZ865 spent some time in the fifties as a racing machine and achieved a creditable second place in the 1950 King's Cup Race. At this time she carried the civilian registration G-AMAU on a fetching royal blue with gold colour scheme a scheme most appropriate to her sponsor, HRH the Princess Margaret. Much of the flying in the race was carried out by Group Captain Townsend who flew Hurricanes during the Battle of Britain.

Below—PZ865 found itself a new job in the early sixties during the development of the Hawker-Siddley P1127 Kestrel, the forerunner of the famous Harrier. The low-speed handling made her ideal as a chase plane for the prototype 'jump-jet' particularly in the transition trials from vertical to normal flight.

The perfect setting? PZ865 sits in a genuine 1940 hangar at Biggin Hill in June 1995. A Battle of Britain aircraft in a Battle of Britain hangar on the premier Battle of Britain station. Dreams are made of this!

Above–September 1994 and PZ865 flies over the rocky coves and inlets of Jersey on the way to the annual Battle of Britain air display held at Jersey airport each year.

Opposite page–The tubular frame of the Hurricane can clearly be seen in this cockpit shot of PZ865. The BBMF actively discourage people from climbing into the cockpits of the aircraft. It's all too easy to lose a pen or other objects in the cluttered cockpits, objects that could easily jam controls with possibly fatal results!

Below–After another display in August 1995, PZ865 is fully refuelled before going back into the hangar. The fuel tanks on all the Flight's aircraft are always kept topped up. If the tanks are full, there is no oxygen for the fuel to combust with. A half-empty tank leads to petrol fumes which are very explosive. When in the BBMF hangar the aircraft are also connected to long earthing cables which reduce the risk of ignition from a build up of static electricity.

On the evening of the VE day celebrations in May 1995, Flight Lieutenant Paul Shenton enjoys the rare privilege of flying Hurricane PZ865 over the centre of London on a beautiful summer's evening. The CAA does not normally allow single-engined aircraft to fly over the centre of London due to the risk of engine failure causing an aircraft to come down in the busy metropolis. Therefore, for special events, aircraft like the BBMF fighters are guided for much of their route over the Thames. If it all goes wrong the pilot is expected to ditch the machine. Happily, this never happened and both the VE and VJ flypasts were carried out without a hitch.

Hurricane Mk IIc LF363

Hurricane Mk IIc LF363 was delivered to no 5 Maintenance Unit on 28th January 1944 and later joined no 63 Squadron where it is believed to have been the last Hurricane to enter RAF service. Before the end of hostilities LF363 also went on to serve with 309 (Polish) Squadron and no 26 Squadron.

After the war she was used mainly as a communications aircraft until August 1951 when she joined no 41 Squadron at Biggin Hill and flew in the annual Battle of Britain Flypast over London. Up to this time LF363 had suffered a number of minor 'incidents' including a wheels-up landing and the canopy parting company during flight. On the 30th September 1955, LF363 was returned to Hawker's for a rebuild before returning to Biggin Hill in June 1956. Along with the Spitfire MkXIXs, LF363 formed part of the original Historic Aircraft Flight established in July 1957. Up until 1959 she always led the Flypast over London on Battle of Britain Sunday, but after the 'Oxo' incident, when the accompanying Spitfire was forced to land in a cricket field, the flypasts were cancelled.

LF363 has appeared in a number of films in her past including *Angels One Five, Reach for the Sky, The one that got away,* and of course *The Battle of Britain.* The high number of flying hours flown during the making of *The Battle of Britain* took their toll on LF363 and she was flown to 27 MU in March 1969 to have her fabric covering replaced. The interest generated by the film led to an increase in the number of displays flown in 1969 and it would be fair to say that this was the year that the BBMF was finally put on a firm footing. LF363 suffered an undercarriage failure at RAF Northolt, near London in September 1976. Happily damage was relatively minor.

On the 11th September 1991 LF363 and the Flight were on the way to the Channel Islands for the annual Jersey Battle of Britain air display. Squadron Leader Martin, an experienced Tornado instructor from Coningsby was flying the Hurricane. The Flight had not long taken off from Coningsby and was in the Wittering area when the Merlin began to behave erratically. At times the engine would produce no power then it would give a burst of full power, and then die away once more.

Sqn Ldr Martin decided to make for RAF Wittering and managed to get LF363 right down to the runway threshold before the Merlin finally gave up completely. This caused LF363 to stall onto the runway, cartwheel and catch fire. At first Sqn Ldr Martin found himself unable to get out of the burning Hurricane, but fortunately the impact caused the cockpit side panel to come loose. He managed to force it open and clamber out of the cockpit. As he desperately ran to get clear of the burning aircraft he thought that his knee pad had gone around his leg because he could only run very clumsily. It was only when he'd run for about 100 yards and collapsed on the edge of the runway that he realised he'd been running with a badly broken ankle! Happily Sqn Ldr Martin made a full recovery and is back flying with the BBMF.

As for LF363, well sadly she was a complete wreck. The fire had completely gutted the aircraft and nothing but the skeletal remains were left of the oldest aircraft on RAF charge. Closer examination showed that the engine, which had only just come back from a major service, had suffered a broken camshaft. A fracture had failed to be detected with the result that sometimes the camshaft was operating normally whilst at other times it was not. The eventual failure jammed open the inlet valves allowing fuel to pour into the cylinders causing the fire.

After much consideration it was decided to restore LF363 to her former glory and the remains were sent to the Historic Aircraft Flight at Audley End. There, due to the advancement of computer technology, the original parts are being prefabricated and LF363 is gradually being rebuilt as, for all intents and purposes, a brand new production Hurricane. Hopefully, she will be seen in the air again sometime in 1996/97.

Above–This photograph, taken soon after the end of hostilities in 1945, shows LF363 in her all silver, doped colour scheme which she wore while working as a communications hack up to 1951.

Below–The caption on this photograph taken in the mid-eighties, when LF363 wore the colour scheme of a night fighter belonging to no 85 Squadron in 1940, is 'Fly BBMF Airlines, all seats are first class!'

The black colour scheme of LF363 worn in the mid-eighties represented a night fighter of no 85 Squadron. The markings VY-X were originally worn by a Hurricane flown by Flt Lt Wheeler in late 1940.

Flt Lt Wheeler was a First World War veteran who joined no 85 Squadron from the RAFVR in 1940. During 1941 he was awarded the DFC and promoted to Squadron Leader. By 1943 he was a Wing Commander in Bomber Command flying Lancasters. He was the commanding officer of no 207 Squadron when he was posted missing on the night of 22nd/23rd March 1944.

Above–This photograph taken in late 1940 shows Flt Lt Wheeler climbing into his night-fighting Hurricane. The bright area in the background is probably a landing flare from another Hurricane. The white dots across the picture are snowflakes reflecting the camera flash.

Battle of Britain Hurricane Wrecked

An inquiry was continuing today into the crash landing which destroyed an historic Hurricane fighter plane from the Battle of Britain Memorial Flight.

The Hurricane pilot sent out a Mayday distress call during a Flight from RAF Coningsby to the Jersey airshow yesterday, The pilot, Sqn Ldr Al Martin was attempting an emergency landing at RAF Wittering near Peterborough, but the plane crashed just short of the runway and burst into flames.

He escaped with a suspected broken ankle and was today said to be comfortable at Peterborough District Hospital.

The Mk IIc fighter, number LF363 was one of two Hurricanes making up the memorial Flight. It was accompanied by the Flight's City of Lincoln Lancaster.

Cambridgeshire police say witnesses reported seeing a fire before the plane landed.

An RAF spokesman said, 'It is a write-off as far as flying is concerned but parts may be salvaged for a static display. Accident investigators have set up a board of inquiry and will be examining the wreckage to try and establish what happened.'

The plane was the older of the two Hurricanes in the Memorial Flight and is believed to have entered service in 1944.

Newspaper cutting September 1991

Vintage fighter may fly again

A vintage war plane which crashed and burst into flames at RAF Wittering last year may fly again.

The World War II Hurricane fighter—one of just a handful left—was badly damaged after coming down at the base near Stamford on its way to a show in Jersey.

The pilot escaped serious injury.

Now plans are afoot to try and re-build what remains of the aircraft, which featured in the classic war films *Battle of Britain, Angels One Five* and *Reach for the Sky.*

The plane is currently at the Battle of Britain Memorial Flight headquarters at RAF Coningsby in Lincolnshire.

A spokesman there said, 'It is in a terrible state but we believe it can be repaired. Everybody wants to see it refurbished. It is a very rare plane.'

But he said an RAF investigation into the cause of the crash will have to be completed before a final decision is made.

September 1992

Below and inset–The burnt-out hulk of LF363 made the return journey to the BBMF hangar at Coningsby on the back of a low loader. As can be seen from the photographs, the damage was extensive leaving only the skeletal remains of the RAF's oldest flying aircraft.

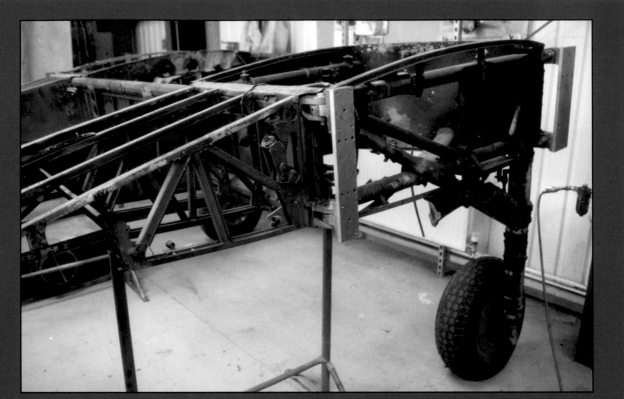

Above– The remains of the centre section of LF363. There will probably be very little of the original LF363 left by the time the restoration is complete. Much of her will have to be scratch built so, to all intense and purposes, she will be a brand new Hurricane. Historic Flying hope that around sixty percent of the new LF363 will be original.

As a founder member of the BBMF and the oldest aircraft still on RAF charge the argument for putting LF363 back in the air were very strong. The Ministry of Defence invited tenders for the rebuild and ways for finding the funding without dipping into the public purse were considered. The contract was finally given to Historic Flying Ltd based at the small airstrip at Audley End in Essex.

Reluctantly the BBMF had no choice but to put one of their Spitfires up for sale to fund the rebuild at Audley End. The axe fell of Mk XIX PS853 which went to auction via Southebys, on 26th November 1994. It was originally sold to a bidder for £410,000, however the sale fell through and some rapid behind-the-scenes negotiations followed. The result was a new buyer in the shape of Euan English, a founder member of the 'Squadron' at North Weald. Sadly, Euan was never to enjoy the benefits of his new purchase as he was killed in a flying accident in his Harvard IIAG. At the time of writing the future of PS853 is uncertain.

Historic Flying is best known for its Spitfire restorations and by the end of 1995 had worked on thirteen Spitfires of which six were restored to flying condition. Created by businessman Tim Routes in 1988, Historic Flying came about from a deal Tim had struck with the MoD to acquire five Spitfires that had been 'gate-guardians' outside RAF bases. The quality and experience gained in restoring these and other Spitfires won Historic Flying the contract to rebuild LF363.

The sad remains of LF363 were delivered to Audley End in September 1994 and is scheduled to be returned to the BBMF in July 1996 in a 'better condition that when she left Hawker's factory in 1944'. As much of the original airframe is being used in the rebuild as possible, however such was the damage caused by the crash and subsequent fire, that in reality much of the rebuilt LF363 will be from new parts.

All the wooden parts such as the fuselage decking, ribs and stringers, were completely destroyed by the fire, and all these will have been replaced. A new radiator, Merlin engine and overhauled propeller unit are being supplied by the BBMF. Much use will have been made in the rebuild of HFL's computer aided machine tools which can generate full sized drawings on film for all the Hurricane parts. This method speeds the rebuilding process up dramatically and ensures parts of superb accuracy including all the positioning for rivets and attachment points.

Above– **The new basic fuselage frame of LF363 awaits attention on the hangar floor of Historic Flying's workshop.**

The first job in the rebuilding of LF363 was to build a Hurricane wing jig. This jig was built with the aid of the wings from the other BBMF Hurricane P7865. Once a completely accurate wing jig was built the work of rebuilding the centre section and outer wing section could begin. The jig alone took three months to build, but hopefully will be used by HFL to rebuild other Hurricanes in the future. The outer wing panels were largely destroyed in the crash so these will be built from scratch and mated to the centre section in the jig. Where possible metal as specified by Hawker's has been used, but as metallurgy has advanced dramatically since the 1930's it isn't always possible to find the original material. In these situations a modern equivalent has been utilised.

If an original Hurricane part can be found and used it will. For example, the original pilot's seat was melted in the fire and after much searching a genuine Hurricane seat was found. It would probably have been quicker and easier to fabricate a new one at HFL but the philosophy is that the more original parts make up LF363 the more original she will feel. This raises the old argument of 'will the rebuilt LF363 be a replica or original Hurricane?' My own answer is that to the pilot LF363 will still feel and fly like a Hurricane. To the public LF363 will be a Hurricane regardless of what the purists may say. If they are that sad as to want to dismiss a superb effort by the HFL team, then they have my sympathies.

*Below–*Historic Flying have wide experience in restoring vintage aircraft and can scratch build aircraft to order. Here can be seen Spitfire VB EP120 nearing completion. This Spitfire took to the air again on 12th September 1995. The jigs used to rebuild LF363 will be used to build more Hurricanes to order. Hopefully the rebuilt LF363 will back in the air towards the end of 1996.

73

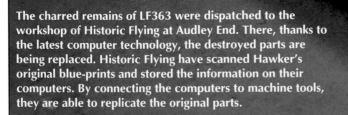

The charred remains of LF363 were dispatched to the workshop of Historic Flying at Audley End. There, thanks to the latest computer technology, the destroyed parts are being replaced. Historic Flying have scanned Hawker's original blue-prints and stored the information on their computers. By connecting the computers to machine tools, they are able to replicate the original parts.

The new main fuselage frame can be seen on the workshop floor. This section is completely new.

LANCASTER PA474

There can be little doubt that the Lancaster was the most successful bomber of the Second World War. Developed from the notoriously unreliable Vulture-engined Manchester, Lancasters made no fewer than 156,000 sorties over enemy territory and dropped a total of 608,612 tons of bombs. Out of an incredible 7,377 Lancasters built, only two remain airworthy: one in Canada, the other being PA474.

Built in Chester in mid 1945, PA474 was delivered to the RAF too late to see action in the European theatre and was destined to join the Tiger Force in the Far East. This force was due to support the invasion of the Japanese home islands, however the dropping of the atomic bomb on Hiroshima and Nagasaki ended the war before mobilisation. PA474 was assigned to no 82 Squadron in East and South Africa. In its role of photographic reconnaissance, PA474 had all her turrets removed and flew in a natural metal finish with the identification letter 'M'.

Life for PA474 was nearly cut short when, on her return to the UK, she was loaned to Flight Refuelling Ltd based at Tarrant Rushton. The plan was that PA474 would be converted to a pilotless drone and if this plan had gone ahead there's no doubt that she would not have survived until today. Happily the Air Ministry decided a Lincoln would be more suited to the task and PA474 was transferred to the Royal College of Aeronautics.

There she was used in tests on the Handley Page Laminar Flow wing. A laminar flow swept wing was attached vertically to the rear fuselage of PA474 and she was used as a flying test bed gathering data on the new wing section.

In 1964 the Air Historical Branch acquired PA474 for display in a proposed RAF museum. She was flown to Wroughton and repainted in wartime colours. Whilst there she took part in two films, *Operation Crossbow*, and the film that seems to be shown every wet Sunday afternoon, *The Guns of Navarone*. After her acting career ended PA474 was moved to RAF Henlow in preparation for display in the new RAF museum at Hendon. In the end R5868 'S for Sugar' was displayed at Hendon leaving PA474 without a home.

On Christmas Eve 1941 three Lancasters were delivered to no 44 (Rhodesia) Squadron, the very first of thousands of Lancasters in squadron service. In early 1965 no 44 Squadron, based at Waddington, was equipped with the latest Avro Vulcan and the CO asked permission for PA474 to be kept at Waddington, in recognition of the squadron's long association with A.V. Roe. An inspection showed that PA474 was still airworthy and permission was granted for one last final Flight from Henlow to Waddington.

In commemoration of John Nettleton who won the Victoria Cross flying Lancasters in the war, PA474 was painted in the markings of 'KM-B' the aircraft he flew in the Augsburg raid on 17th April 1942. Over a period of years no 44 Squadron undertook a full restoration of PA474 and by 1966 both the front and rear turrets were back in place. However, a mid-upper turret could not be found anywhere. In 1967, PA474 finally took to the air again.

After flying with no 44 Squadron for a few years, PA474 was transferred to the renamed Battle of Britain Memorial Flight in November 1973, still in the colours of 'KM-B'. A mid-upper gun turret was finally found at an air gunnery school in Argentina of all places and was brought back to the UK aboard HMS *Hampshire* and fitted to PA474 in 1975, the year she was adopted by the City of Lincoln.

For the VE and VJ celebrations in 1995, PA474 wore the markings of 'WS-J' Johnnie Walker, an aircraft of no 9 Squadron. This aircraft took part on the first attack on the battleship *Tirpitz* and flew over 100 missions.

Lovingly cared for and adored by everyone, PA474 may never have seen hostile action, but she is a beautiful and fitting tribute to the other 7,376 Lancasters built, and all who flew them.

Right–Lancasters of no 82 Squadron sit in the baking sun in their natural metal finish at RAF Eastleigh, Nairobi, 1951.

PA474 was given the letter code 'M' and served with no 82 Squadron in the photo-reconnaissance role.

Left–PA474 at the Royal Aircraft Establishment, Cranfield in 1963. Like so many Lancasters, PA474 was used as a flying test bed. The extra fin set vertically on the fuselage is a laminar flow swept wing designed by Handley Page. Other Lancasters were used to test new jet engines and avionics.

Above–Once placed safely in a hangar at RAF Waddington, PA474 underwent a restoration that took several years. By 1966 work was progressing well and, as can be seen from the photograph above, a front turret had been refitted. The original was removed when she flew with no 82 Squadron in Africa.

On Tuesday 7th November 1967, PA474 took to the air once more after restoration by no44 Squadron. Painted in the markings of 'KM-B' flown by John Nettleton VC, PA474 was ready in time for RAF Waddington's fiftieth anniversary.

The test Flight was carried out by Group Captain Arthur Griffiths, Sqn Ldr Ken Hayward (800 hours on Lancasters) and Chf Tech Ken Terry (thirty WWII ops in Lancs). The first post-restoration flight lasted seventeen minutes.

Above–Photographed from a chase plane, PA474 flies above the clouds collecting data on the laminar flow wing in 1963.

This photograph, found in the BBMF scrapbook, is believed to have been taken in August 1965 when PA474 was flown from Henlow to Waddington. There is some doubt as to who the smiling chap in the cockpit is, but the note scribbled on the original photograph says it is Flight Lieutenant Niezerecki of Polish nationality.

At this time PA474 had her natural metal finish replaced with a wartime camouflage paint scheme, but without squadron markings. In the previous year 1964, she was used in the making of two war films, *Operation Crossbow* and the better known *Guns of Navarone*. After a period at RAF Henlow where PA474 was to be prepared for display at the new RAF museum at Hendon, the CO of no 44 Squadron sought and got permission for PA474 to be flown to RAF Waddington. No 44 Squadron was the first unit to be equipped with Lancasters on 24th December 1941.

From:- Group Captain K.P. Smales, DSO, DFC, RAF

Air Attache
British Embassy
Buenos Aires
Argentina
10th April 1967

JN Wortley, ESQ
35, Watts Lame,
Hillmorton,
Rugby,
Warwickshire.

Dear Mr Wortley

Mr Broad has shown me your letter to him of February 13th, 1967, and I have passed on your good wishes to Diego Kenny who, incidentally, retired from the Air Force a few weeks ago and now has a good position with the Directorate of Civil Aviation.

Of course I know Mike D'Arcy very well, he was one of my students at the Staff College and I took particular interest because I myself commanded 44 Squadron between May 1942 and January 1943, and you may have seen that a member of the Royal Family is to present a standard to the Squadron at Waddington on Thursday 15th June this year. I doubt whether I shall be able to get back for it, but I shall try. Of course, John Nettleton was one of my Flight commanders soon after I took over the Squadron and after he had done the Augsburg raid.

And now about your turret. I have arranged that the turret and any other bits and pieces connected with it will be shipped from here in HMS 'Kent' the guided missile cruiser of the Royal Navy which will be visiting here in July and will arrive back in the UK, probably Portsmouth but I will let you know in mid August. I should think you could get RAF transport to meet it.

So far I have had no success with the two inboard propellers and a set of ignition harness, but I have every hope.

With my best wishes,

Yours sincerely,

Ken Smales

Right –Well the turret did finally arrive from Argentina, but it was delivered onboard HMS *Hampshire*, not HMS *Kent*.

The Argentine Air Force flew Lancasters just after the war and the turret was rescued from their air force instructional school. There it had been used for ground turret training.

The turret was refurbished and finally fitted to PA474 on 26th March 1976. Happily the airframe structure contained the ring for the turret even though one had never been fitted before. After a short test Flight the then Lancaster captain, Sqn Ldr Ken Jackson, said there were no problems with the turret at all.

80

Left–6th November 1974 and PA474 is completely stripped down for a major overhaul at RAF Kemble. 'Does anyone know how to put this thing back together?' Happily someone did.

This photograph comes from the BBMF archives and is labelled on the reverse side: 'The reason why PA474 didn't fly in 1978. All rivets in the main plane changed by no 71 Maintenance Unit RAF Abingdon.'

Apparently magnesium rivets were used a lot on Spitfires and at some stage were fitted to PA474. The problem with these rivets are that they react with aluminium over a period of time and corrode away. The corrosion can get so bad the rivets can be pulled off with your fingers! So PA474 was grounded for the 1978 flying season whilst no 71 Maintenance Unit replaced all the rivets with the 'correct item'. There is another school of thought which says that the exhaust gases from the engines caused the corrosion—which explanation is actually correct is unclear. The photograph shows the underside of the starboard main plane trailing edge.

Operation Hamburg

No106 squadron RAF Coningsby 26.7.1942

Entry from the Flight log book of Sergeant Naylor, mid upper gunner on board
Lancaster J-Jonny on the night of 26th July 1942.

Above–Three Lancasters drone on towards Germany in this rare wartime colour photograph shot in 1942.

The crew:-

P/O Wellington- Pilot
P/O Bone - Navigator
Sgt Goodwin - F/Engineer

Sgt Webster - W/OP
Sgt Naylor - Dorsal Gunner
Sgt Cunningham - Bomb Aimer
Sgt Needham - Rear Gunner

Take-off and outward journey rather uneventful. Whilst making bombing run over target, hit by flak causing over 500 holes in starboard wing and in forward part of the fuselage. Sgt Goodwin was badly wounded in the neck. Sgt Cunningham was badly wounded in the base of his spinal column. Sgt Webster was wounded in the right hand. P/O Bone suffered from temporary shock. The flak hit was of the flashless variety and knocked the a/c from 12,000ft to 4,000ft.

When plane was pulled out from dive the starboard outer petrol tank caught fire and made an aiming mark for the Hun A/A (anti-aircraft gunfire). On testing my turret controls I found that the hydraulics had been shot away rendering my turret ineffective. On making another run up on the target it was found that the automatic release for the bombs (a full load of incendiaries) had also been rendered useless. I tried to release the bombs manually but there was no joy. By this time we were being buffeted around the sky by flak bursts.

After a while we were coned by 300 searchlights (approx.). Whilst we were coned every uninjured member of the crew noticed a strong smell of burning. On investigation we found the bomb racks were on fire. Sgt Cunningham although wounded, opened up the front hatch and leaned out of the plane and played a fire extinguisher over the bomb racks (the amusing part about it being that at first Sgt Cunningham got hold of the wrong end of the extinguisher and received some of the chemical contents in his face with the aid of the slipstream). This act was successful. P/O Wellington put the a/c into a steep dive and this resulted in the petrol tank conflagration being extinguished.

P/O Bone was suffering from shock still and we were hopelessly lost. While flying round aimlessly we were attacked from astern by a lone Focke Wolf 190. Sgt Needham fired a short burst and the Hun wasn't seen again. The attack was so sharp that I could not get my guns to bear manually.

Things were quiet after the attack for about one hour and then P/O Bone called over the intercom that we should be over England. Someone spotted an aerodrome with perimeter lighting and a green aldis giving us the tip to land.

We made all the preparations to land and got down to 1,000ft. Then we were greeted a thick concentration of light flak (obviously a stunner). Taking evasive action violently we managed to evade the flak and the pilot gave us the order to bale out. The reason being that the plane was in danger of dropping to pieces any moment. Everyone elected to stick with it, so eventually we made a sticky landing at Coningsby with a tyre punctured and a full bomb load. The plane J-Jonny had done six hours flying prior to that trip and was written off as scrap.

Above –Another gem from the BBMF archives is this colour photograph of a Lancaster minus its squadron codes. The unmarked photograph was probably taken in 1942 at about the time of Flight Sergeant Naylor's epic flight.

On a hot day a lovely breeze flows along the fuselage if the escape hatches are left open.

The firing arc of the rear turret is very wide and it needed to be. The rear turret gunner was far more likely to fire his guns in anger than the dorsal turret gunner. As most of the Lancasters operations were at night, the dorsal turret became somewhat redundant and was removed from the modified Lancs carrying the 'Tallboy' earthquake bombs and the 'Dambusting' bouncing bombs.

The view from the dorsal turret is superb and it needed to be. In this shot Hurricane PZ865 peels away. In wartime it would more likely be a Focke-Wolfe or Messerschmitt. A simple roller and guide inhibits the guns when the fin and tailplane are in the line of fire.

First Flight in a Lancaster

Squadron Leader Rick Groombridge leant over and tapped me on the knee. I looked at him through slightly dazed eyes—it had been another long 'socialising' session in the BBMF mess and the 'Elephant' beer brought back from Ostend on the Dakota the weekend before was taking its toll.

'Warren, I hear you haven't had a ride in the Lancaster yet,' he stated. I nodded back dumbly. 'Well we can't have that,' the Boss continued. ' Ted when's the next available slot on the Lanc?'

'August the 20th Boss,' Ted replied.

'Well make sure Warren's on it will you?' the Boss commanded.

'Will do Boss,' Ted confirmed. Paul Shenton looked at me and grinned; it was his doing.

The morning of Sunday 20th August 1995 arrived with no clouds in the deep blue Lincolnshire sky, little to no wind and like most days that summer, the prospect of being very, very hot. It was the second day of the VJ celebrations and another busy day for the BBMF.

Bleary eyed, I traipsed down the stairs and headed straight for the pot of black coffee. Paul was already sitting in the garden soaking up the sun's warmth looking irritatingly well groomed in his all-black flying suit. Paul was scheduled to fly the Hurricane for an hour that morning and was already prepared. I collapsed into the garden chair next to him, still feeling slightly fragile. In the background I could hear the girls talking in the bathroom. The evening before had been good fun; Paul and his better half Louise had been out to dinner with my better half (also named Louise) and myself. As usual the evening had degenerated wonderfully with me knocking back several whiskies before hitting the sack, the only downside being that the whiskies were now playing kettle drums in my head. Paul looked at me and said dryly, 'You look like hell. You'll be sick.'

'Not me,' I replied.

'Trust me,' he countered, 'the Lanc will be boiling in this weather and the mid-upper turret is the hottest spot of all. You'll be sick.'

'Not me Paul. I'm a glider pilot, I'm used to being thrown around the sky.' As soon as I'd said it I regretted it. There was me telling a Tornado and Spitfire pilot that I knew a thing or two about being thrown around the sky! What a plonker! I looked up from my coffee at Paul. He was grinning at me knowing that he'd succeeded in winding me up. I grinned back. The girls arrived and we piled into the car.

One hour later and I'm sitting in the changing rooms at RAF Coningsby. I've got my green flying suit on (they wouldn't give me a black one) and a survival instructor is fiddling with my green kevlar 'bone dome' helmet.

'How does that feel?' he asks.

'What? I can't hear you!' I shout back like an idiot. He pulls a little lever on the back of the helmet and suddenly hearing is restored.

'How does that feel?' he asks again.

'Oh, fine,' I reply in a more sensible tone.

'Okay you'll do,' he says and together we march back to the BBMF hangar. 'You know,' he says to me in confidence as we cross the Tarmac, 'you get these 56 Squadron pilots in being kitted out and they're arrogant bastards. Some of them, mentioning no names, fly for the BBMF, but when they come over to get kitted out for flying the Lanc, Hurri or Spit they're the nicest guys you can meet. They're pleasant and jokey. Funny that. Means something.'

'What?' I asked.

'Dunno,' he replied, 'but it means something. The Boss, Rick Groombridge, nicest bloke you could meet. He came over one day and it must have been obvious that the 56 boys had been giving me a hard time, 'cause he

88

City of Lincoln

Above–PA474 is a little unusual in that it has a second yoke for a co-pilot. Of course, during the war there was only one pilot and it was fairly common practice for other members of the crew to be unofficially trained to fly the Lanc at least straight and level. If the pilot was mortally wounded, then it was up to the others to haul him out of the seat and do their best to bring the beast home.

came over while I'm in the middle of kitting out, puts his arm around me shoulder and says, "These Tornado blokes, all a bunch of pansies. Couldn't fly a real plane to save their lives," and walks off. Creased me up—great bloke.'

We arrived at the BBMF hangar and my escort waved and left with a 'have fun'. I'd already had my briefing, been genned up on all the emergency procedures so I walked straight over to the Lanc and climbed aboard with the help of Sergeant Paul Blackah and Sergeant Keith Brenchley who were in charge of the passengers that day. My spot on PA474 was to be the mid-upper turret. To climb up into the turret you place your foot on a tubular step that swings out from the side of the fuselage. I needed Keith to help me up so I could easily imagine what fun the gunners had when fully laden with flying kit. By the time I'd hauled myself up into the turret, sweat was dripping into my eyes so I wiped it away with a corner of my flight suit and arranged myself as comfortably as possible on the leather belt that went under my buttocks and hooked onto the side of the turret. It was a surprisingly comfortable seat, for now. What it would have been like after an eight-hour mission was another matter. The view from the turret was superb. I had a full 360 degree view. I could see the cockpit, four Merlin engines, masses of wing in front and the twin fins and tailplane behind.

Before I knew it the four Rolls-Royce Merlins had roared into life and we were taxying to the end of the runway. I gave a quick wave to Paul Shenton and made myself as comfortable as possible. Flight Lieutenant Jerry Ward, the co-pilot, called up on the intercom to make sure everyone was secure.

'Bomb aimer secure?'

'Bomb aimer's position secure.'

'Navigator secure?'

'Nav's position secure.'

'Wireless Op secure?'

'Wireless secure.'

'Mid-upper secure?'

That was me. 'Mid-upper position secure,' I replied.

'Tail gunner secure?'

'Tail gunner's position secure.'

The Merlins rose to a roar, the brakes were released and PA474 began to accelerate down the runway. The tail rose and before we had even used half of Coningsby's runway, the Lancaster rose into the air. The climb to 1,000 feet was brisk and the Hurricane and Spitfire were soon tucked in close formation. I waved to 'Uncle' Squadron Leader Chris Stevens in the Hurricane. On the way to the first turning point I examined my new environment. The two hydraulic levers, which in wartime would have controlled the traversing of the turret, weren't operative, but I found a small hand crank in the centre of the gun mount, below the breech block. I gave it an experimental couple of turns and hey presto the turret rotated! Now we were going to have some fun!

I rotated the turret until the guns pointed forward, noticing that as the turret passed through the beam, the drag of the guns in the airflow caused me to put a fair amount of effort into the crank.

With the guns forward I was rewarded with a nice blast of air, which helped to cool me off. In this heat it was a tonic, but during the winter, at night, I bet the gunners got bloody cold! From this position I could see all along the top of the fuselage to the cockpit and out to each wingtip, with the four Merlins roaring away. It was a superb view! Somebody popped their head up into the astro dome and grinned at me, I grinned back and he took a photo. The city of York appeared on the horizon and I heard the navigator call out, 'four minutes to turning point'. Then I heard a curse from the pilot, Flight Lieutenant Mike Chatterton, 'Damn, did you get that? They're late finishing the service, we're on hold for twenty minutes.'

'Okay,' came the cool response from the navigator, 'we'll go into holding position over Elvington airfield.' The Lanc banked to port and we started doing large lazy circuits around Elvington airfield. About 1,500 feet below I saw a group of modellers with their radio-controlled aircraft look up and wave from the runway of Elvington. I waved back with amusement. I've done a fair bit of radio-controlled flying myself over the years and it always looks odd when you see a model from the air. Quite a few time I've mistaken them for a moment for full-size machines. Goodness knows what they thought of a full-size Lancaster circling above them. I rotated the turret towards the tail as PA474 once more headed towards York cathedral and watched the huge deserted airfield of Elvington slip into the haze.

We were almost on top of York by the time I got the turret pointing forwards again and we were descending rapidly. A river flashed by and I heard 'That's the turning point there, where that group of people are on the bridge', then they were gone. The Flypast was completed and I'd not even got a chance to see the Minster, it

Below–The radio operator's position was the warmest position in the Lancaster; all those valves giving off heat meant that the wireless operator was often sweating when the rest of the crew were freezing.

91

all happened so quickly! However I was sure it looked very impressive from the ground.

PA474 climbed back up to 1,500 feet and headed off towards the coast. I felt a pull on my leg and looked down to see Keith peering up at me. He wasn't connected to the intercom, and there was no chance of us

making ourselves heard above the din of four roaring engines and a 150 knot slipstream. However, from his hand gestures I figured he wanted me to climb down from the turret, which I did with some reluctance. Somebody else wanted the best seat in the house, so I guess it was only fair that I gave somebody the chance to rotate the turret. Keith gestured towards the rear turret. Did I want to play 'tail-end-Charlie' for a bit? Did I ever! Together we clambered down the rear fuselage, clambered being the operative word because the interior of the Lancaster seems designed to bruise knees, elbows and any other unfortunate part of the anatomy that gets in the way. The Lanc's bomb bay ends

Above–The coastline by the Humber bridge slips below the rear turret. just aft of the mid-upper turret and there is quite a sharp drop down to the fuselage floor before it rises again towards the rear gun turret. In fact the whole of the interior of the Lancaster is one huge obstacle course with a massive mainspar to climb over to get to the cockpit, and a tiny squeeze to get down into the bomb aimer's position. Getting past all this was difficult enough during the day with light pouring in through the open escape hatches (left open to get extra ventilation down the inside of the fuselage) and me wearing just a light flying suit. Imagine what it must have been like at night, with full flying kit and the plane being thrown around the sky by flak!

Eventually I squeezed myself feet first into the rear turret. It was a tight fit with my head constantly hitting the metal frame at the top of the turret. Keith tapped me on the shoulder and gave me the thumbs up. I returned the gesture and he battled his way forward again past the long lines of ammunition belts that lay in trays on each side of the fuselage and fed the four Browning machine guns of the rear turret. The view from the rear turret wasn't as good as that of the mid-upper. You can only traverse the turret until it lines up with fin port and starboard while the breeches and mount of the four machine guns obscure a lot of the view, but there is a good clear view panel in the perspex directly in front of the gunner. There was also a good breeze which was greatly appreciated, and a wonderful smell which was a mix of aviation fuel, machine oil and metal; the smell of a 'real' aeroplane! Sitting with your back to the rest of the aircraft watching the world slip past the tail you feel very remote. During the war, tail-end-Charlie's must have been very short and very lonely sitting there in the dark with nothing but a bit of perspex and four Brownings to protect them from attack.

As I finally got myself comfortable in the cramped turret, PA474 crossed the Humber bridge and headed south once more. The huge girders of the bridge raced under the turret as did numerous pleasure boats out enjoying the hot weather. Then to my surprise a sea mist obscured the view and all I could see was a blanket of white cotton wool speeding below us, bright and intensely white in the sun that shone down from a blue sky above. For the first time I felt a sensation of speed, it felt as if PA474 was a speed boat skimming the crest of white-capped waves. I looked up and saw the Spitfire and Hurricane still in close formation. 'Uncle' in PZ865 must have seen me because he rocked his wings; I waved back.

Above–The main spar is a major obstacle that has to be climbed over to reach the cockpit.

After half an hour PA474 turned back inland and the sea mist disappeared so that once more I was looking down on a patchwork quilt of brown fields and villages disappearing under the guns of the turret. Coningsby roared by underneath as we swept by in the traditional fly-by before pulling up into circuit. With a thud the undercarriage locked into the 'down' position and the note of the Merlins changed. I watched as the shadow

Above–The BBMF hangar disappears below the rear turret as PA474 does a fly-by before joining the Coningsby circuit.

of PA474 swept over Tattershall castle, then the threshold of the main runway appeared complete with black tyre marks from the numerous jets that scream into Coningsby. With a slight jolt and screech the main wheels touched down and she decelerated rapidly. Being a tail dragger, the Lancaster drops back onto the tail wheel as she loses speed giving the tail-end-Charlie a very close view of the ground. It was an interesting viewpoint!

We taxied back to the BBMF hangar, stopped, and one by one the engines shut down and a strange silence descended upon PA474. She was no longer a fire breathing, noisy, vibrating flying machine. She was asleep once more with only the pinking of cooling metal to remind you of the sheer brute power that had kept her flying only minutes ago.

Paul and the girls were standing at the edge of the perimeter track. I waved and Paul took a photograph. Then with some sadness I unplugged my intercom lead and hauled myself out of the tiny confines of the turret. I climbed up the fuselage to the crew hatch and stepped down the ladder. With some difficulty I pulled off my 'bone dome' helmet and shook my head. My ears were still ringing. Louise came up and gave me a hug. Paul took the helmet out of my hands and said, 'Well, were you sick?'

I looked at him with a grin that stretched from ear to ear and replied, 'Nah, not me mate!'

Above–PA474 is refuelled at Biggin Hill airshow 1994. When operating away from the BBMF home base at RAF Coningsby, groundcrew go with the aircraft to refuel and service them. When the Lancaster, Spitfire and Hurricane perform a display together the groundcrew travel in the Lancaster. On some trips the fighters are escorted by the Dakota. If the fighters are appearing alone the groundcrew will travel by road.

Below–The Merlins roar into life outside the BBMF hangar at RAF Coningsby in August 1995. A crowd of onlookers stand at the fence. There always seems to be an audience whenever there is an aircraft movement. Note the fire extinguisher always kept close to hand when engines are started.

Above–North Weald 1995, B-17 'Sally B' and a trio of 'little friends' roar over PA474 as she taxies towards the runway at the start of her slot. The airshow season starts in April and ends at the beginning of October. The BBMF appear at over 200 events each year, far more than the other RAF display team, the Red Arrows.

Below–Biggin Hill airshow, June 1994 and a Nimrod does its display in glorious blue skies over a parked PA474. Biggin Hill is where the BBMF started with the Historic Flight back in 1957. The ex-RAF Battle of Britain station is now a centre for civil and business aviation but still retains many of its wartime hangars and buildings.

September 1995 and Lancaster PA474 flies low over the coastline of the Channel Islands enroute to the annual Battle of Britain airshow at Jersey airport.

DC-3 Dakota ZA947

Built in February 1942, Douglas Dakota ZA947 was initially issued to the US Army Air Force. She was then transferred to the Royal Canadian Air Force (RCAF) in September 1942. In 1944, ZA947 served with no 164 Squadron, RCAF at RAF Manston in Kent. She flew with the RCAF in Europe up to the end of the war and carried on as a work-horse until 1969 when she was finally retired. Through the 1960s ZA947 served with 109 Flight RCAF based at Grostenquin in France. With the disbandment of the Flight in 1969 ZA947 was stored at Prestwick, Ayrshire.

At that time the Royal Aircraft Establishment (RAE), based at Farnborough, had been using a Dakota but theirs was nearing the end of its useful life. ZA947 was purchased as a replacement aircraft by the RAE and allocated the serial KG 661. Her work for the RAE included launching remotely piloted vehicles and dropping sonobuoys through holes cut in the fuselage floor.

There was some doubt about the serial number KG 661. Research showed that a Dakota serialled KG 661 had in fact been destroyed in an accident while on active service in 1944. There was probably some confusion with the serial 661 used by the RCAF. So the serial number was changed to ZA947. In her years with the RAE ZA947 was often used to demonstrate parachute dropping.

In 1992 the Defence Research Agency who succeeded the RAE declared her surplus to needs and offered ZA947 for sale. Strike Command acquired the Dakota on behalf of the BBMF and she joined the Flight in March 1993. Refurbished by Air Atlantique at Coventry, ZA947 is painted in the colours of an aircraft flown by no 217 Squadron in 1944. The original aircraft was flown by Flight Lieutenant David Lord over Arnhem in September 1944 for which he was awarded a posthumous Victoria Cross.

The acquisition of the Dakota has led to the retirement of the BBMF De Havilland Devon. This aircraft was used as a liaison and training machine, carrying groundcrew and equipment when the Flight operated away from Coningsby. However, there have been problems with operating the Dakota in this role. Its cruising speed is too low to keep up with the fighters, and being a tail-dragger aircraft it has a fairly low crosswind limit. Being that much larger than the Devon, it also cannot fly into some of the small fields that the fighters operate from.

In a perfect world the Flight would like to operate both the Dakota and the Devon. It seems unlikely that funds will be made available to do this, so for the time being ZA947 will have to carry out the liaison/training role alone.

Above–ZA947 flies over the city of Lincoln during the D-Day celebrations in June 1994. The Dakota is used as a display item herself, representing the thousands of 'Daks' used by transport command during the war. ZA947 also carries more navigational aids than the other aircraft on the Flight which allows transit in civil airlanes. However, the Dakota is not the ideal escort aircraft. Her cruising speed is a little too slow for the fighters whereas the retired Devon was able to cruise at 175 knots which is a more comfortable pace.

Below–July 1995 and ZA947 starts her Pratt & Whitney engines. Flt Lt Jerry Ward is the pilot and the passengers are VIPs from NATO on a visit to RAF Coningsby. It's a relatively straightforward job for seats to be bolted to the interior of the Dakota and ZA947 fulfils a useful role as both a VIP passenger aircraft and a load carrier.

Above–ZA947 taxies out for her own display slot at the 'Fighter Meet' at North Weald in May 1995. Throughout the world there are still hundreds of Dakotas still in operational service. Her rugged construction and ability to carry heavy loads out of rough airstrips makes the 'Dak' the ideal transport aircraft for more remote parts of the world. Large numbers of Daks were sold to South American countries after the war. Many of them are still in service, particularly in Colombia where for many remote towns and villages they are the only practical means of transport and supply.

Once allocated to the BBMF, ZA947 was sent to Air Atlantique at Coventry Airport to be overhauled. Air Atlantique operate a fleet of Daks and have wide experience in operating and servicing Dakotas. After a major service ZA947 was flown to RAF Marham where it was repainted in the wartime colours of an aircraft serving with no 217 Squadron at the time of operation 'Market Garden', the airborne assault on Arnhem in September 1944. The markings YS-DM belong to the aircraft flown by Flt Lt David Lord who was shot down on 19th September 1945 and was awarded a posthumous Victoria Cross.

Right–The BBMF practices dummy parachute drops during the run up to the fiftieth anniversary of D-Day.

During the war paratroopers would be connected to a static line. This line would be attached to the Dakota so that when the paratrooper leapt out the rear fuselage doors the parachute would be automatically deployed.

In modern warfare the paratrooper has largely exchanged his parachute for the troop-carrying helicopter.

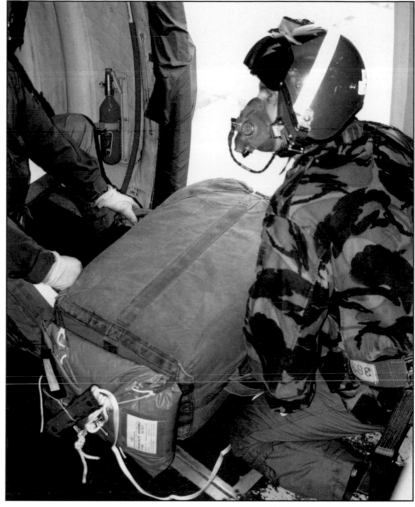

Below–ZA947 proves she can still carry a 'useful' load. This time the pallets strapped to the interior of the fuselage carry kegs of beer for the BBMF mess!

103

Winter 1994 and ZA947 flies over the snow covered fields of Wiltshire practising parachute drops. Once a year the BBMF Dakota crew pactice parachute drops. This allows the Flight to remain current and drop parachutists at displays and commemerations such as the anniversary of D-Day and Arnhem. The Dakota was the main work-horse of the parachute regiments and transport command during the war.

De Havilland Canada Chipmunk WK518

The De Havilland Chipmunk was designed as a replacement for the famous Tiger Moth which was the wartime basic RAF trainer. Designed by Wsiewolod Jakimuik, a Polish aircraft designer who fled the Nazis in 1939, the Chipmunk was the first original design by the Canadian offices of De Havilland. 255 Chipmunks were built in Canada and another 1,014 were built in the UK. The first examples entered RAF service in 1950.

Thousands of pilots and members of the Air Training Corp will have had their first Flight in a 'Chippie'. Delightful to fly, the BBMF Chipmunk WK518 is painted in the colour scheme of a basic trainer based at RAF Cranwell during the late 1950s. WK518 was first delivered to RAF Cranwell in January 1952 and has logged over 10,800 hours air-time since then in numerous University Air Squadrons and with the BBMF.

The Chipmunk serves several important roles in the BBMF. Firstly it is used to keep pilots current on 'tail-dragging' aircraft, particularly out of season when the rest of the Flight is being serviced. New pilots first fly twenty-five hours in the Chipmunk when they join the Flight, before moving on to Boscombe Down's Harvard and then the Hurricane. All BBMF pilots must fly five hours in a 'tail-dragger' each month and the Chipmunk is available for this purpose. The Chipmunk is also used to check out new air display locations before the arrival of the Lancaster and fighters.

The De Havilland Chipmunk is now being withdrawn from RAF service, the last examples at Air Experience Squadrons being replaced by Bulldogs. This means that the BBMF Chipmunk itself may well become a display item in years to come.

Above–Displaying the classic De Havilland fin shape, the Chipmunk was designed as a replacement for the Tiger Moth as a basic trainer in the RAF after the war. A delight to fly, the BBMF 'Chippie' is used to keep pilots current on 'tail draggers'.

Right–The Chipmunk has a four-cylinder, air-cooled Gypsy Major engine. Of all the aircraft on the Flight, the Chipmunk is undoubtedly the simplest to work on. Having said that, 1995 was not a good year for WK518 and the 'Chippie' was often unserviceable due to a number of small complaints.

The De Havilland Chipmunk is now being retired from the last air experience flights still operating the type. The Bulldogs which are replacing them are not considered ideal due to the fact that it's necessary to cut the engine before the next cadet can leap aboard. This is a problem the 'Chippie' didn't suffer from. There are also complaints that the poor young chaps who fly air experience tend to be a little on the short side to reach the Bulldog's controls.

Engineering

Maintaining aircraft designed and built in the 1930s and 40s is a real labour of love. During the war the aircraft of the BBMF were at the leading edge of technology, although they are not considered sophisticated by today's standards. However, trade skills that were once commonplace have now all but disappeared, as have all the thousands of spare parts that were available at one time. This means that the small group of RAF engineers that volunteer for duty on the BBMF not only have to learn many of the necessary skills on the job, they have to be expert at tracking down elusive and rare spare parts.

With the BBMF appearing at over 200 events each year the engineers often find themselves working long hours ensuring that the aircraft are serviceable. As an example, PA474 dropped hundreds of poppies over the SS *Canberra* as part of the D-Day celebrations in 1994. Just three days before the event the Lancaster suffered an engine failure shortly after take-off. The engine was shut down and the Lancaster landed back at Coningsby. Upon inspection it was found that the Merlin had suffered an internal failure and had to be replaced. Usually, this would take seven days, but the engineers had to complete their work in three! The fitters worked twelve-hour shifts and called in all their favours from other trades. On the morning of 5th June 1994 PA474 joined one of the Spitfires and a Hurricane for the Flypast.

The BBMF engineers are all devoted to their charges. When you discuss an aspect of the aircraft, their eyes light up and they talk as if the aircraft were living, breathing machines with characters of their own. The atmosphere as you enter the hangar is professional but relaxed. The engineers enjoy a close working relationship that they feel is sometimes lacking in the rest of the modern Royal Air Force. They work hard and play hard. After a long shift, they will often join the pilots on a 'bender' in the local pub helping to bond the relationship between flyer and fitter. When the BBMF is on a 'stopover' at another airfield, members of the groundcrew will go with the 'road show' to service and look after the aircraft. Away from home base the pilots rely heavily on the skills of the fitters when one of the planes has 'teething problems' and the bond amongst the members of the BBMF becomes even stronger.

As the years go by spare parts become more and more scarce. Warehouses full of spare parts for the Merlin, Spitfire, Hurricane and Lancaster have long disappeared. If a piece can't be obtained from the BBMF stores it has to be begged, borrowed or bartered from somewhere. Some spares come from other vintage 'warbird' collections. There is a lot of cross fertilisation of information and parts between the BBMF and such groups as the Fighter Collection, or Old Flying Machine Company at Duxford. Parts often come from 'donations'. Over the years anything from Merlin engines to propeller spinners have been donated by supporters of the BBMF who have come across the parts in scrapyards, old hangars, barns and numerous other sites.

Increasingly, as the years go by, it becomes harder and harder to find genuine spare parts. However, due to the marvels of modern technology it is possible to replicate parts on computerised machine tools. This method of part production is becoming more popular and the rebuild of Hurricane LF363 relies heavily upon the ability to produce parts that are exact reproductions of the original. As the BBMF moves towards the 21st century, it is likely that more and more spares will be produced in this manner.

Without the dedication of the engineers and fitters of the BBMF the Spitfires, Hurricane and Lancaster would be no more than dusty, grounded hangar queens.

But more than that, it is the personalities that are the engineers and fitters and their relationship with the aircrew that really make the Battle of Britain Memorial Flight. The combination of a close working team, aviation fuel, oil, metal, dope and well-worn leather is a heady cocktail that is a living memorial to all the men and machines that served in the wartime Royal Air Force. One could not exist without the other!

Below–Tim Coulson turns over the engine of Hurricane PZ865 during routine maintenance. Much of the engineer's training is 'on the job'. The RAF stopped training engineers on the intricacies of piston engines many years ago, so it is necessary for a new member of the groundcrew to learn his skills from an 'old sweat'.

Above–Although major servicing is carried out on each aircraft in the BBMF during the winter, it is sometimes necessary to remove an engine during the airshow season. In July 1995 the Mk V Spitfire AB910 had to have her Merlin removed following a serious oil leak. The fault was traced to worn bearings in the supercharger casing which sits at the rear of the Merlin. If left unattended the bearings would have eventually failed with very serious results—the complete seizure of the engine!

Below–It took SAC Dave Ford and Corporal Nigel Bunn over a week to replace the bearings and refit the Merlin. That's why the BBMF is keen to maintain the number of aircraft on its charge. If a Spitfire becomes unserviceable there is always a spare, ensuring airshow organisers and the public are not disappointed.

110

1978 and AB910 has her cockpit stripped out for a major overhaul.

Above–Corporal Fiona Holding refuels PM631 from a bowser. After each flight the aircraft are refuelled. It's safer to keep the aircraft in the hangar with their tanks full. Petrol fumes in half-empty tanks are very explosive, but if they are kept topped up there is no air in the tanks so reducing the fire-risks.

Below– July 1995 and AB910 has her Merlin removed following a serious oil leak. Corporal Nigel Bunn and SAC Dave Ford have traced the problem to worn bearings in the supercharger casing.

Maintained with loving care and attention, PA474 gets a good hosing down in 1983.

Above– With her cowlings and spinner off PA474 sits outside the BBMF hangar after a primary service. The 'Johnnie Walker' nose art is clearly visible as is the inscription 'Still Going Strong'. The markings are that of a Lancaster of no 9 Squadron which on its 100th mission dropped a 'tallboy' bomb on the German battleship *Tirpitz* in Alten Fjord, Norway on the 15th September 1944.

Below– Three of her four Merlins removed for maintenance, the Lancaster sits outside the hangar during a winter servicing schedule. During wartime it was rare for a Lancaster to be brought into a hangar. Nearly all the servicing was carried out at dispersal points around the airfields regardless of the weather conditions. The life expectancy of the aircraft was so short that corrosion caused by the elements was never considered a problem. It was rare for an aircraft to complete a full 'tour' of missions.

Apart from the couple of weeks it took to carry out 500 and 1,000 hour overhauls, wartime Lancasters rarely saw the inside of a hangar. The wartime Lancasters lived their lives on the ground at dispersal points spread around airfields, often several miles from the main hangars and buildings. About twenty-eight Lancasters completed the magic 100 operations. The exact figure is a little obscure due to the transfer of aircraft from squadron to squadron, the discrepancies between log books and squadron records and the sheer number of aircraft in service.

The code WS-J, the markings PA474 wore for the 1995 season, come from a no 9 Squadron B1, W4964. 'Johnny Walker' began her career in April 1943 and completed her 100th operation on 15th September 1944, dropping a 12,000lb tallboy bomb on the Tirpitz in Alten Fjord, Norway.

On returning to RAF Bardney, the pilot, Flt Lt Doug. Melrose, and his crew were presented with a crate of 'Johnny Walker' whiskey. After completing 106 trips WS-J was pensioned off and finally scrapped in 1949.

115

Above–With engine cowlings and spinner off , AB910 shows her Merlin engine and plumbing to good effect.

There are four levels of servicing for the BBMF aircraft. The first level is the 'primary' which is carried out after thirty hours air-time (the number of hours spent in the air), or every four months, whichever comes first. During the winter the fighters are given a 'star primary' which is a step up from the summer routine. Every other winter the fighters are given a 'minor' servicing and every sixth year they go away for a 'major' service.

On average a 'major' service takes some 2,500 man-hours for a fighter and 7,500 man-hours for the Lancaster. If this work were to be carried out by the BBMF itself, it would stretch their resources to the limit. Therefore major servicing is contracted out. During the winter of 1995, PA474 went to RAF St Athan to be stripped down to the bare bones by RAF engineers to have her main spar removed. The spar was then renewed by British Aerospace clearing the way for the Lancaster to continue flying well into the 21st century.

The servicing schedule is based upon wartime experience, however there is a much lower number of flying hours between servicing than would be required for modern aircraft. During the war, it wasn't expected that many aircraft would survive long enough to require a 'major' service.

The original maintenance manuals have been rewritten in a format the current BBMF groundcrew are more familiar with, which makes life for the new technician a little easier.

PA474 is stripped down for maintenance in 1983. During the winter of 1995/96 the Lancaster underwent a major operation to have her main spar replaced, ensuring her airworthiness well into the 21st century

Above–Hurricane PZ865 has her side panels removed for inspection. The Hurricane with her many removable panels is far easier to service than the Spitfire. During the Battle of Britain it was common for parts from several wrecks to be put together to form one complete Hurricane, something that could be achieved far more easily than with the Spitfire.

Below–After another long day, Lancaster PA474 is towed back into the BBMF hangar.

Left–PM631 gets a good polish from Corporal Fiona Holding after a sortie in July 1995.

When the aircraft are stripped down for servicing, many of the vital parts, such as crankshafts in the engines, and main spars are X-rayed and stress tested. This enables a comprehensive assessment of the condition of the aircraft. Plans can then be made to replace any parts that are nearing the end of their useful life.

The aim of this is to solve potential servicing problems before they occur so ensuring safe operation. However, even with these modern inspection methods a major component failure can still occur as was the case with the fractured camshaft in the engine of Hurricane LF363.

The offending camshaft in LF363's Merlin had been recently X-rayed by a private contractor, however, it still failed quite spectacularly.

Today the BBMF work very closely with the CSDE—the Non-Destructive Testing Squadron, based at RAF St Athan.

Below–The cowlings are removed from PA474 for access to the Merlin engines during a primary service in 1994.

119

Aladdin's Cave

The now largely derelict airfield of RAF Woodhall Spa was once the home of 617 Squadron, the 'Dambusters'. Most of the old hangars and buildings are gone and the runway is overgrown and partially ripped up. A haulage and aggregate firm now occupy the spot where Lancasters ran their engines up before setting out on missions deep into enemy territory. However, tucked away in one corner, out of sight from the main road, is a building, a modern building whose exterior appearance gives no indication as to its

Corporal Druid Petrie stands beside a hoard of new Lancaster Tyres.

use. There's a small fence around the building and two members of the RAF Regiment guarding the single entrance. I followed Corporal Druid Petrie into the innocuous building through a side door. It was cool and dark inside in stark contrast to the sticky July heat outside. There were no windows, the only light coming from the open door.

'Druie' walked over to the light switch and flicked it on. Suddenly the interior was bathed in light and what I saw took my breath away. The interior of the building was huge with rows of shelving that reached to the high ceiling. Stacked neatly as far as the eye could see were boxes and boxes of spare parts. Druie walked over to the first row of shelving and picked up a box at random. It contained valve stems for Merlin engines. I picked up a crankshaft for a Griffon engine; it was still covered in packing grease and the label on the end was dated February 1945.

This Aladdin's cave is where the BBMF keeps all its spare parts, from nuts and bolts to complete engines. 'This place is a collector's dream,' said Druie. 'There are people who would do anything to get their hands on some of this stuff.'

'Where did it all come from?' I asked in awe.

'All over the place really,' came the reply. 'Some of it comes from original RAF stock. Some of it is donated from the original manufacturers while other bits come from the back of old barns, hangars, wherever. Of course we occasionally have to get new parts made. Come and look at this.' Druie led me to a collection of huge tyres stored against one wall. 'Spare tyres for the Lanc,' he said. 'We asked Dunlop if they could make a spare pair, but we ended up having to buy a load. There's enough here to last well into the next century.'

'I had no idea you had such a store of parts,' I said looking at a spare spinner for a Hurricane. 'How many of the original wartime spares can you still use? Don't they deteriorate over a period of time?'

'Not really,' he replied. 'The wax-oil they used to preserve the parts is very effective at keeping out corrosion. Before we use a part it's normal to get it stress tested and X-rayed. Quite often we get given parts that have turned up on scrap heaps or in the back of someone's garage.' Druie pointed to a battered Merlin engine in a corner: ' That one came from a private donation. You can see where a hole has been punched in the crankcase to drain the oil and that means that water will have got in. Even so, we'll strip it down and remove any parts we think we can clean up and use again.'

Row upon row of neatly stacked spares.

'This place is amazing!'

'Isn't it just,' Druie finished herding me out the exit. He switching the light out and locked the door once more sealing the BBMF Aladdin's cave. I felt very privileged to have seen such a treasure trove.

120

Above–Winter 1980 and Hurricane LF363 is stripped down for a 'primary star' service.

A lot of the major servicing is carried out by RAF St Athan, South Glamorgan. Operating on a commercial basis, the RAF's own maintenance unit has successfully competed for BBMF contracts in the face of rival bids from industry.

The Lancaster PA474 underwent a major service at St Athan over the winter of 1993/94 and the 'baby' Spitfire P7350 also underwent a 'major' over the winter of 1994/95. The extent of the work undertaken in these services is considerable with a 'major' on the Lancaster taking twenty skilled technicians anything up to six months. Over the winter of 1993, the Lancaster was completely rewired and all her engines, fuel tanks and turrets removed for inspection.

British Aerospace have a library of original drawings for the Lancaster and these were used to working out how to re-wire PA474.

Above–Spare props for the fighters. The blades of the propellers are constantly checked for signs of damage or fatigue.

Above–Winter 1983 and PZ865 wearing her original markings of 'The Last of the Many' is also given a 'primary star' service.

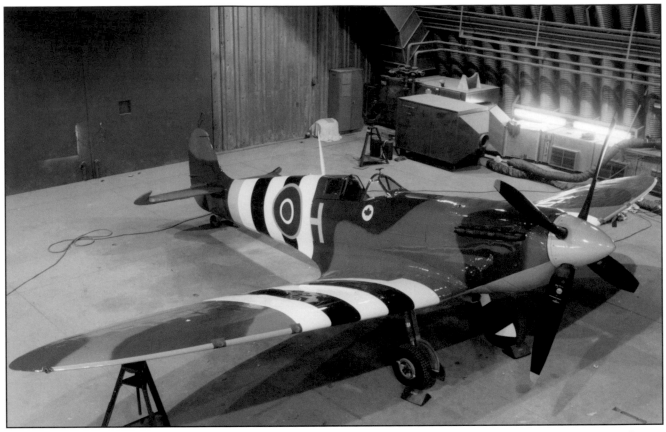

Above–Every few years the markings on the BBMF aircraft are changed, usually after a major service. Here AB910 receives a new colour scheme and markings.This time the markings are AE-H which come from a Spitfire flown by the Canadian no 402 Squadron on D-Day the 6th June 1944. All the BBMF aircraft are painted in a gloss polyurethane paint which was believed to provide better protection for the airframes and be easier to maintain. Of course, during the war the finish was matt rather than gloss and, at the time of writing, the BBMF had just been given permission to repaint the aircraft in a more authentic matt finish. The belief that gloss paint protects the airframe would appear to be no more than common myth!

Above–Although the Merlin engine was considered the height of technical advancement at the time it was produced, it is simple compared to modern jet engines. However, as the RAF does not train any of its engineers on piston engines any more it is necessary for new technicians to the BBMF to learn their trade largely on the job. It can take months for new technicians to get to the stage where they no longer need to constantly refer to the operations manual or one of the 'old sweats'.

Opposite–When an engine suffers from an internal failure, metal can be turned into an oily pulp in seconds, just as with this derelict Merlin engine. It took SAC Dave Ford and Corporal Nigel Bunn over a week to replace the bearings and refit the Merlin out of AB910. That's why the BBMF is keen to maintain the number of aircraft on its charge. If a Spitfire becomes unserviceable there is always a spare.

Above– Merlin engines appear from a number of sources including scrap yards and the back of people's barns and garages! This one is covered in wax-oil to preserve it and may well one day find itself powering a Spitfire, Hurricane or Lancaster.

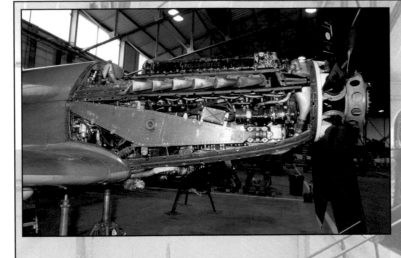

'You have to learn on the job. At ground-school they only teach you what a propeller looks like and what a piston engine is. Then they say that a jet turbine is better than a piston engine because, and that's it. You learn everything here from scratch. '

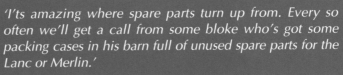

'I'ts amazing where spare parts turn up from. Every so often we'll get a call from some bloke who's got some packing cases in his barn full of unused spare parts for the Lanc or Merlin.'

'They reckon that the AV gas will run out before the planes wear out.'

124

'They're supposed to keep the tools on a board all together, so none of them go missing. But they never do. They just spread them all out on the floor where it's easy to reach down and grab what they need.'

'It's very relaxed here, the officers and non-coms get on really well and will have a beer together. People from other squadrons can't get their heads round that. Officers are officers and non-coms are non-coms, but that simply wouldn't work here. We all have to muck in together.'

'These have got to be the most over-serviced aircraft in the RAF.'

The BBMF hangar at RAF Coningsby photographed from the bomb bay of Lancaster PA474.

'The civilian Spitfires have all got chips in the paintwork and oilstains all over them. It's a question of money but I guess they must be okay because they've all got their C of A.'

'I love working on these machines, but I'm not so sure about the flying. It's not so bad now, but I used to get really airsick. I find that if I sit in the tail turret it doesn't affect me so bad. There's a gap at the back there, and the fresh air keeps me going.'

'You have to be so careful with dropping things in the cockpit, especially the Hurricane. If you drop a pen or anything, you can be sure it will foul up the controls. That's why we're so cautious about people getting in the cockpits.'

'We have to earth all the planes (using cables to the side of the hangar). We never used to bother because every time they land, the charge that builds up in the air is discharged through the tail wheel. It's the new Chief. Because every other aircraft in the Air Force is earthed, then these have to be too. He plays it by the book, but then AV gas is very volatile, so maybe it's not such a bad idea–just in case.'

THE PEOPLE

As you walk into the BBMF hangar at Coningsby the first thing you notice is the smell. That heady scent of oil, aviation fuel, dope and well-worn leather is as unmistakable now as it was during the 1940s. The next thing that strikes you is the presence of the aircraft. These warriors of a bygone era, lovingly cared for, have a grace and beauty that belies their purpose.

Yet as they sit in the hangar there is something missing, something that stops these machines from being anything more than a collection of museum pieces. The hangar is quiet, the aircraft unmoving, dead, waiting for someone to bring them to life. Then a member of the groundcrew emerges and turns a propeller over by hand. Other groundcrew walk onto the hangar floor, stride over to one of the waiting machines and push it past the open hangar doors and into the warm summer sunshine. A pilot casually strolls up to the vintage machine and looks her over with a practised eye. Satisfied, he hauls himself up onto the wing and clambers into the cockpit. A member of the groundcrew helps him with his straps.

The pilot goes through his pre-flight checks, then satisfied all is well fires up the Merlin engine. Life returns, the heart of the old warrior beats again–no longer is the machine a museum piece. The collection of old metal and fabric once more becomes an aircraft. The pilot taxies the beast to the end of the runway, the engine is revved up and the aircraft roars down the runway and leaps into the air once more.

The groundcrew hold their hands to their brows to shield their eyes from the strong sunlight and watch their pride and joy roar through her natural element. The warrant officer turns to one of the groundcrew and says, 'If you do that again, I'll really lose my rag.'

The groundcrew turns and shrugs his shoulders, 'What did I do?' The warrant gives him a dirty look and walks away. There are the rest of the aircraft to prepare for the weekend's sorties. This scene actually took place during the long hot summer of 1995, the fiftieth anniversary of the end of the Second World War, but it could just have easily have been any moment in time taken from the war.

This is the essence of the Battle of Britain Memorial Flight, a place where life continues as it did in the past. not a museum, but a way of life. What is it that creates this magic timewarp? Is there something in the aircraft themselves? Do they somehow bestow upon those that tend them, the souls of all those who flew and maintained the aircraft in years gone by? Can memories been ingrained in an airframe or engine?

I don't have the answer to these questions, nor I suspect does anybody else. However, there is one thing of which I am sure–at a time when the RAF is suffering from low moral and lack of purpose, it is the BBMF and the people who are part of it who keep alive the real soul and history of the Royal Air Force. And that is something a collection of nuts and bolts alone cannot achieve. The Battle of Britain Memorial Flight is the sum of its parts–take away the Spitfires, Hurricanes and Lancaster and you have an empty hangar. Take away the people, the characters, the pilots, groundcrew and support staff and you have a collection of lifeless museum pieces.

Right–The BBMF appear at over 200 events each year and for many people they represent the Royal Air Force's 'finest hour'. Young and old alike become spellbound by the roar of Merlin engines

Opposite–While AB910 sits on the apron at RAF Coningsby, Squadron Leader Paul Day climbs into Spitfire PS915 on a Flight test prior to the start of the airshow season.

128

INTERVIEW WITH THE BOSS, SQUADRON LEADER GROOMBRIDGE

What's your personal history Boss?

As a boy I was evacuated to the South Coast near Tangemere. So I watched all the fighters fly from there. Then after the war I worked on a farm near there and watched Neville Duke in his red Hunters and all the other test pilots who were making attempts at the world speed record. So that was it for me, I was going to be a test pilot. So I got pre-selection at Cranwell at fifteen and a half, then I foolishly fell in love with a girl who said she would not marry a fighter pilot so I said to the Air Force 'I'm not interested'. Then the young lady and I split up so there I was working in this bank, bored stiff, so I went back to the Air Force and said 'I want to be aircrew now' but there were no aircrew jobs.

National service was coming up for me so I joined up early as an air radar mechanic, but in fact I eventually became a Russian interpreter. I was commissioned as a flying linguist in Shakletons doing intelligence work, but I got fed up because as a linguist we would land somewhere exotic and I was getting my twenty-eight shillings a day, while the flying officer aircrew was getting four pounds a day. So I applied for aircrew. Got off to a good start in training and got my wings. I then applied to fly heavies, because I liked the Shakletons, but the powers that be said no. Because I'd flown the Meteor and Vampire in training, they sent me to CFS as an instructor. After that I flew Lightnings, then went on exchange with the French Air Force flying Mirages from 1972-74. Then I came back to the UK to fly the Phantom in air defence.

I left the Air Force in 1977 because my career was going so well I would have had to fly a desk in a few more years. So I went on contract to Saudi Arabia, instructing on StrikeMasters. After a while the Air Force got so short of people I came back in on a special deal just flying aircraft, nothing else. I came back to Phantoms and Tornados, and went to the Gulf War with a Saudi squadron. In the end I was there two years. This time when I came back to the UK I came back to Coningsby as a simulator instructor, then when they offered me this I said yes. Mind you I'd turned it down twice before. When I volunteered I thought of fighters but I got a thing back saying 'you'd be perfect for Lancasters'. But I've always been a fighter pilot. The first two times I was offered the BBMF I was flying my bum off in the operational conversion unit. I love fighters, but you've got to be fair and let the youngsters take over.

I'm enjoying this job but there is an awful lot of responsibility and a lot of leeway for screwing up. I'm here because I thought it would be more demanding than vegetating in the simulator. It's one hell of a challenge. You've got old aeroplanes that can't fly in the cloud and they've all got a 10 knot crosswind limit and you've got at an airshow 60,000 people waiting to see the BBMF and I'm the one who has to say we can't do it. We're not interested in showing how good the pilot is. We're showing them to the public. We show the aeroplanes off to their best advantage.

What's the story behind the Devon being 'retired'?

The Devon is very sad. Basically we are under pressure from a particular senior person, he's the only one—he keeps saying everyone knows he's the BBMF's best friend, but we know he isn't. He is trying to have the Flight cut by half i.e. down to three fighters, which Paul Day and I reckon would mean the end of the Flight. He's got our four yearly review, and he's saying that we've all got to economise and that when we get the Hurricane back we'll have six fighters. He's already made us sell one to finance the restoration of LF363. So when we get the Hurricane back, he wants us to mothball three, but that would reduce the number of shows we can do by half. Frequently we have three teams of two fighters going out and most certainly wouldn't have any spare aircraft. At the moment we manage to fly at 75-80% of the events we are asked to attend. It's usually weather that stops us rather than aircraft going unserviceable. If they mothball half the fighters there won't be any spare fighters for us to leap into.

Squadron Leader Rick Groombridge joined the RAF in 1958 and transferred from his posting as a Russian linguist to pilot in 1961. Since then he has flown continuously as a Qualified Flying Instructor (QFI). His log book contains numerous types including the Vampire, Meteor, Lightning, Mirage III and V, the Phantom and Tornado F3. The 'Boss' has over 250 hours on the Lancaster and 6,500 flying hours in total. He took over the position as Officer Commanding the BBMF from Squadron Leader Tomalin at the beginning of 1995.

During the winter when the Lancaster is in for a service we used to go to Lossiemouth and train on the Shakletons, but of course all the Shakletons are gone now. So the RAE (Royal Aircraft Establishment) had this great idea that we should have their Dakota which is good practice during the winter. Unfortunately the Dakota is too slow to keep up with the fighters. It's also got a crosswind limit because it's a tail-dragger and you need a large handling party on the ground. So you can't take it into all the fields that you can take the fighters into, whereas with the Devon, me and the nav can just push it out, take-off and land anywhere. The

Dakota also costs money. If it goes unserviceable then it costs big bucks and spares have to come in from the States. Where as with the Devon all the spares are here in this country. July is the end of the review period and the chances are that the Devon would be sold which is very sad. So not only have we been forced to sell the Mk IX Spitfire, we'll also have to sell the Devon which is a real shame.

At the end of the Second World War they took the ricksaws and power saws to all the bombers. End of war, don't need anymore weapons of war, was the attitude, which is why there is only one Lancaster still flying.

'For a lot of people, what they see of the RAF when they go to airshows is the BBMF. '

They kept the Spitfire and Hurricane because they were the defence fighters but even they were going for the chop. When they brought in the Meteors and Vampires a bunch of guys said 'Here that's not on! We've got to keep some of these old fighters flying!' and it was these guys just at weekends with a few voluntary engineers that got the whole thing going. Then eventually it got the name the Historic Flight, which later became the Battle of Britain Memorial Flight. But even then it was the same guys giving up their weekends, no Officer Commanding the BBMF or anything. All the flying they did at airshows made them very popular so after a lot of hard work in 1973 they got the Lancaster from no 44 Squadron at Waddington and that's when it became the Battle of Britain Memorial Flight. From there on in they put the whole thing on a more official footing.

Today I am the only permanent guy. In essence I am the Battle of Britain Memorial Flight with the help of Yvonne and Ted. That's it–everybody else is a volunteer, they all give up their weekends. The groundcrew are all on detachment from Engineering Wing, now we do three times as many displays as the Red Arrows, this year we are doing 394 aircraft events, so we're in great demand, but with no real back-up, although we have lots of friends and they help us keep everything going.

There is an ex-air marshal who used to fly with the BBMF and now flies for the civilian Fighter Collection based at Duxford. It's my fear that if the worst happened, our aircraft would be sold to the Fighter Collection and of course this guy is qualified to fly all our aircraft. You see, if you were a display organiser and we had only three aircraft flying, you would think twice about booking the BBMF because we wouldn't have the numbers of aircraft flying to meet all our commitments. So you would book the Fighter Collection instead because they could meet the commitments. So after a couple of years interest in the BBMF would diminish, and then you'd get some accountant at MOD saying, 'well public interest has dropped, it's been more than fifty years, let's sell off the BBMF'. If that happened who would have the money to buy all the aircraft? Who could have a pilot qualified to fly all the aircraft? It would be the Fighter Collection.

I've got nothing against that–in a way it might be better that the BBMF were privatised, but it shouldn't be. It's part of the Air Force, part of our heritage.

June 1995

Right–North Weald in May 1995 and the 'Boss' discusses the forthcoming display slot with co-pilot Flight Lieutenant Jerry Ward and the rest of the Lanc crew.

For a lot of people their first point of contact with the Battle of Britain Memorial Flight is Yvonne Walker and Ted Farrant. They provide the administration and support that ensures the aircraft arrive at the airshows on time, try to accommodate Flypasts over village fetes or reunions and arrange visits for those with a special interest in the Flight. Ted is a retired Flight Lieutenant who in thirty-four years of service as an Air Electronics Officer, flew 8,500 hours in eleven different aircraft types. Yvonne joined the Flight in 1993 from the Supply and Movements Squadron at Coningsby.

Without their support the BBMF would rapidly grind to a halt. Their office is a hive of activity every day, looking like a wartime operations room. Requests for airshow appearances start to flood in as soon as the flying season is over and it is their job to juggle the various dates to try and accommodate everybody. Of course last minute alterations can cause havoc to this careful organisation and once the flying season starts they are constantly under pressure to keep the flying schedule from sliding into chaos.

By each Christmas the basic layout for the following season's appearances is prepared and detailed planning beings in earnest in the New Year. There are certain airshows, such as Biggin Hill, Jersey Airport and Mildenhall that are long-standing major events, all other events are considered by the Participation Committee at the Ministry of Defence who decide where all the forces' major display teams, such as the BBMF and Red Arrows, should appear. Whenever possible, if smaller events coincide with larger airshows, the Flight will try to do a flypast on the way in or out of the main display. The display season starts in April and ends in September by which time the Flight will have appeared at up to 300 venues.

During 1994 and 1995 the BBMF took on a new significance as they appeared in the D-Day commemorations in June 1994 and the VE and VJ commemorations in May and August 1995. At these internationally important events the Lancaster stirred the hearts of thousands with her 'poppy drop'. The bomb bay of PA474 was filled with red 'poppy petals', the recognised symbol of remembrance for the war dead, and as the Lancaster roared over the Solent and the Mall in London, the bomb bay doors were opened and a huge cloud of bright red petals floated to the ground. The significance of a heavy wartime bomber dropping a symbol of peace and remembrance rather than tons of high explosives can not be underestimated.

There is some concern that with the end of the fiftieth anniversary commemorations of the Second World War interest in the Battle of Britain Memorial Flight will start to wane, particularly as more and more warbirds are being displayed by private groups such as the Fighter Collection. At the time of writing there are nearly fifty Spitfires in airworthy condition around the world, however, it costs a lot of money to book a privately owned warbird. The BBMF can and will appear at worthy events regardless of the size of the display organiser's bank balance, so ensuring that the general public always get to see the RAF's 'jewels of the sky'.

AIRCREW

Above–'Uncle' Squadron Leader Chris Stevens sits in the cockpit of Spitfire P7350 and contemplates the rain. The Biggin Hill Airshow in June 1995 was an unfortunate washout and was even more unfortunate considering not another drop of rain fell anywhere until September! Conditions such as these are extremely marginal and 'Uncle' told me afterwards that if the Biggin Hill Tower hadn't called his slot off, he would have been forced to cancel it himself. In 1994 the BBMF flew at 254 venues out of a scheduled 294, the others being cancelled mainly due to poor weather conditions.

You might imagine that the BBMF is deluged with applications from Top Gun pilots all wanting to fly the aircraft of the 'few', but that isn't the case. The reason for this is really very simple flying for the BBMF is a huge commitment. You see, all the pilots and aircrew that wheel the RAF's 'jewels in the sky' at hundreds of airshows each year are volunteers. That means that they still have to complete their squadron duties, which in a typical week might amount to dozens of flying hours in the Tornado or hours in the simulator, paperwork and numerous other tasks. Only then can they go and fly for the BBMF, which of course has its stresses, especially during the height of the airshow season. Aircrew can find themselves flying every day of the week for long stretches at a time fulfilling their commitments to their squadron and the BBMF.

Sitting in the comfort of your armchair you might think, 'Huh—I wish I was flying Tornados and Spitfires seven days a week!' Well in theory it sounds like flying paradise, but the reality is somewhat different. Airshow flying and combat flying (regardless of whether it's training or for real) are very stressful, both require meticulous planning, split-second timing and a high standard of flying skills. All of which take their toll on the body and soul. It's no wonder that after a long week on duty, only a 'few' volunteer for the BBMF.

This doesn't mean that the quality of pilot that joins the Flight is anything but the best. Applicants are carefully chosen, usually from the pool of instructors at RAF Coningsby. Once chosen they then have to complete a carefully structured training programme. New pilots first have to fly the Chipmunk for twenty-five hours to gain experience in 'tail-dragger' flying. Then they are sent to Boscombe Down, Wiltshire, where

Above–Squadron Leader Chris Stevens sits in the cockpit of AB910. Better known as 'Uncle', Sqn Ldr Stevens joined the RAF in 1965. After gaining his wings he spent three years at RAF Valley as an instructor on the Gnat. 'Uncle' then converted to the Lightning and spent the next fifteen years flying the infamous interceptor with no 5 and 29 Squadron and the Lightning Training Flight. With the withdrawal of the Lightning from service he became one of the first four crews to convert to the Tornado F2 at BAE Warton in 1985. He has been on the Tornado Operational Conversion Unit since then. He has a total of over 6,500 hours flying time in his log book. 1995 was his seventh and last season as a BBMF pilot.

they fly in their North American Harvard, itself a veteran design from the Second World War. Once they have completed this stage of the training they are sent solo in the Hurricane PZ865. The reason for this being that the Hurricane has a much wider, robust undercarriage which makes her more forgiving in landings and take-offs. The thicker wing makes her more stable in Flight and the Hurricane is generally regarded as more 'forgiving' than the Spitfire.

After a minimum of fifteen hours in the Hurricane it's time to move on to the 'baby' Spitfires, which are the Merlin-engined Mk II P7350 and the Mk V AB910. Generally the first Spitfire solo is carried out in P7350. Once again the Merlin-engined 'baby' Spitfires are considered to be more forgiving than the larger, heavier Griffon-powered Mk XIXs. The Griffon-engined Spitfires are far more powerful than the Merlin-engined variants, and this extra power means a lot more torque which can be quite a handful, especially on take-off. After another fifteen hours on P7350 or AB910 the pilot can then move up to the Mk XIXs, but this usually occurs in the second season's flying.

Throughout the year the Chipmunk is available for practice in 'tail-dragging' flying and it's necessary for the pilots to fly five hours a month on this type of aircraft to remain current.

Above–Flt Lt Jerry Ward sits in the pilot's seat of PA474. Jerry joined the RAF in 1979 and flew Jaguars and Canberras before converting to the Tornado F3. During the Gulf War Jerry served on no 43(F) Squadron at Dhahran in Saudi. He has a total of 2,800 flying hours in his log book of which 1,250 are on the Tornado. 1995 was Jerry's first season as the Dakota captain and Lancaster co-pilot. During his first season with the BBMF Jerry rapidly gained a reputation as an 'Arthur Daley'. If anything could be sold to add to the BBMF Fund, then Jerry would sell it. The BBMF's gain is the commercial world's loss!

Strict limitations are placed on the operations of the BBMF aircraft with a view to keeping airframe fatigue to a minimum. The fighters are limited to manoeuvres of up to +3G with a never to be exceeded limit of +4G. Inverted flying is also forbidden as the carburettors fitted starve the engines of fuel when inverted causing them to cut. Display routines tend to be made up of wing-overs and barrel rolls rather than the loops and more exuberant aerobatics of the privately owned warbirds.

The Lancaster is limited to just +1.8G and also has a fatigue meter fitted in the cockpit which records stress on the airframe. This can then be analysed later to determine wear and tear on the airframe.

Above–Squadron Leader Paul Day. The Major is very much the 'fighter pilot's'-fighter pilot. He has flown fighters since 1963 having logged 2,000 hours in the Hawker Hunter, 3,000 hours in the F4 Phantom and over 1,000 hours in the Spitfires and Hurricanes of the BBMF. He is probably the world's most experienced Spitfire pilot still flying. The nickname 'Major' comes from the rank he was given whilst serving a tour of duty with the USAF. Not a person to suffer fools gladly, he is the BBMF fighter leader and an awe-inspiring figure.

Airspeeds for the BBMF aircraft are restricted to 275 knots, once again with a view to keeping stress on the airframes to a minimum. The amount of added power provided by the superchargers on the rear of the Merlin and Griffon engines is measured in pounds per square inch and these are restricted to +6 for the Merlins and +7 for the Griffons. Although this restriction in the power settings means that the BBMF is not able to perform those large loops and vertical rolls that other less restricted warbirds are capable of, there is still a large reserve of power. Without the added weight of guns, ammunition, bombs and large valve-radio gear the BBMF fleet are very light compared to the weight of wartime aircraft.

Above–Flight Lieutenant Phil Palmer is one of the Lancaster pilots and 1995 was his second season with the BBMF. Phil has a total of 5,600 flying hours in his log book since joining the RAF in July 1971. He is an ex 'V' force pilot having flown the Avro Vulcan with no 617 'Dambusters' Squadron and no 35 Squadron based at RAF Scampton. In 1985 he moved to RAF Marham where he flew Victor Tankers with no 55 and no 57 Squadron. Phil moved to RAF Finningley to fly the Dominie and then to RAF Coningsby in 1993 where he joined the Operations Wing.

The Lancaster is allowed ten hours' flying time each year for the training of its aircrew. This is obviously not as much as the pilots would really like, so further training is carried out in the Dakota. The Dakota being a large tail-dragger itself, is well suited to this role although it is said to be easier to handle than the Lancaster. Once competent in the Lancaster, each pilot must have his display routine cleared by the Station Commander and the Air Officer commanding 11 Group.

A good example of how the Lancaster can be tricky to handle was given at the Mildenhall air display in May 1992 when PA474 ran off the runway and onto the grass in a strong crosswind. The same thing happened at Brussels in 1994 and the undercarriage legs had to be sent to Dowty for checking. Because of the problems that taking off and landing in a crosswind can cause there is a strict crosswind limit imposed on all the BBMF aircraft. This is 15 knots for take-off and 10 knots for landing. Since these two mishaps, the BBMF have been in touch with some veteran Lancaster pilots to pick up a few tips on the art of landing large tail-draggers, something that has been somewhat lost in the modern Air Force with its nose-wheel aircraft.

A typical Lancaster display routine would include a low flypast with the bomb-bay doors open. There then follows several well-banked turns showing both the topside and underside of the Lancaster. Flaps and undercarriage are then lowered for a dummy approach before rejoining the fighters. Safety is the paramount concern all the time and the display is carefully orchestrated so that the aircraft never over-flies the crowd line.

Above–The long hot summer of 1995 and the team pause during an airshow for a family photo. From left to right–Flt Lt Colin Fryer, Crpl Fiona Holding, SAC Danny Smith, JT Paul Taplin, WO Len Sutton, Crpl Simon Hingley, Loadmaster Mick Clabby, Flt Lt Jerry Ward and Flt Lt Paul Shenton. On this particular trip the Dakota proved its load carrying capabilities by hauling large quantities of 'Elephant Beer' back to the BBMF mess!

Sometimes, such as with large two-day airshows, it's necessary for the BBMF to land for a night stop. When this happens it is the duty of the airshow organisers to arrange hangarage for the Spitfire and Hurricane, although the Lancaster and Dakota can remain in the open. A good example of the need for this was the Biggin Hill airshow in June 1995 when the heavens opened and the rain poured down! Hurricane PZ865 and the 'baby' Spitfire P7350 were kept dry in an original Battle of Britain hangar, on the farside of the airfield.

During these overnight stops groundcrew go with the aircraft to support them. Usually they fly in the Dakota or the Lancaster, although if necessary they will travel by road. Originally the DH Devon fulfilled the support role, however this has now been replaced by the Dakota. Unfortunately the Dakota is not the ideal support aircraft that you might first suppose, the problem being that the cruising speed of the Dakota is quite a lot less than that of the fighters which have a problem flying in formation with the Dakota on transit flights.

Whenever possible the Flight flies directly to a venue so as to reduce flying times to a minimum. Air traffic control have become used to clearing routes for the usual formation of Hurricane, Lancaster and Spitfire although the odd light aircraft can still wander too close to the Flight for comfort. These transit flights are always VFR (Visual Flight Rules) and usually flown at an altitude of between 2,000 and 3,000 feet. The fighters carry no navigational aids which with the busy airlanes over the UK can make long cross-country navigation challenging. With arrivals at air displays timed to the second, traditional map, ruler and stop watch navigation is not really practical for the fighter pilots, so on long flights they rely on the Lancaster or Dakota to shepherd them.

SPITFIRE SOLO

Above–Thursday 28th June 1995 and Flight Lieutenant Paul Shenton finally realises his lifetime ambition and prepares for his first Flight in a Spitfire. As Paul straps himself into the cockpit Sqn Ldr Day checks over P7350, the 'baby' Spit.

Paul Shenton talks about flying the Spitfire for the first time.

Warren— So Paul, how did you feel today when you knew you were finally going to get to fly the Spitfire?

Paul— I suppose I knew right from the day I joined the Flight that this was going to happen. But today, well it's funny because it wasn't as nerve racking as the day I first flew the Hurricane. Flying the Hurricane for the first time, even after flying the Harvard was a little bit tense. I mean the Hurricane was so bloody noisy, so big, so heavy. The Spitfire I expected to be not so noisy which was exactly how it was–the Mk II is a bit rattly on the ground and there are lots of little noises as you trundle along. The view as you taxi is nowhere nearly as good as the Hurricane.

W— Is that a problem, because I noticed that nobody helped you out as you taxied to the runway?

P— No not really. You just 'S' taxi as you go along and look out the sides.

W— Did Squadron Leader Paul Day do the pre-Flight inspection? I noticed he was prodding and giving everything a good look over.

P— Yeah he did that to save time, which was why we didn't hang around once I was strapped in–which was the first time I've ever strapped myself into a Spitfire. In fact it was only the second time I've ever got into the cockpit of a Spitfire.

W— Really? Wow, what was that like?

P— Yes! It was pretty cool! (Laughs) Anyway the Major (Paul Day) watched me do the checks, made sure everything was all right, then I primed the engine, fired her up, but I didn't think it was going to start for a while. It seemed to turn an awful lot before she started. It's funny but the Hurricane always seems to start a lot quicker–I don't know why. (Grabs a beer from the fridge and opens it.) Well I gave it eight primes because it was hot, maybe it could have done with another couple–I don't know. It fired up in the end.

W— So there you were all strapped in and the Merlin is fired up ready to go. What was going through your mind then?

P— It's going to happen–Oh my God–It's going to happen! No–really–it was a nice feeling. Nowhere near the same sort of apprehension as when I first flew the Hurricane.

W— Well was your stomach tense? Did you have the butterflies?

P— Not really, you have to have a practical approach to it. You look at the Spitfire from the outside and you think wow, that's fantastic, but as soon as you get in the cockpit you have to have a pretty practical outlook with only a little bit of romance. The whole thing is a baptism of fire.

Above–Flight Lieutenant Paul Shenton strikes a pose beside the Hurricane in the summer of 1995. He joined the RAF in September 1986 from a University Air Squadron. After completion of flying training on the Jet Provost and Hawk he was posted to no 25(F) Squadron at RAF Leeming flying Tornado F3s in 1990. Paul moved to RAF Coningsby in October 1993. He has over 1,000 hours in the F3 and 1995 was his first season with the BBMF where he soon gained the nickname 'Shagger'. He is also a good friend of both authors with whom he has downed much Elephant beer and discussed the finer points of flying in the traditional drunken manner.

W— So you got to the end of the runway. What then?

P— Once I was there I was completely happy with the checks, so that wasn't something that I had to worry about. I had a quick look around the cockpit left and right to make sure, trim, propeller and everything was in the right place. Then I put the power up–it was a lot quieter (than the Hurricane).

I didn't really have to lift the tail, I didn't get the chance before the bloody thing was airborne. It gets airborne so quickly. Once on climb out I had to do this stupid thing with

Above–With a puff of white smoke the Merlin engine roars into life. The weather was so hot that day, there was some concern that the engine might overheat if P7350 didn't get into the air fairly rapidly after the engine had been fired up.

changing hands to retract the undercarriage (the undercarriage lever is on the right-hand side of the cockpit on the Spitfire which means the pilot has to change hands on the control column to reach the lever–definitely not desirable on take-off!). So I got the gear up with a certain amount of PIO (pilot induced oscillation)–it's a lot lighter on pitch than the Hurricane–then climbed away. I got to 7,000 feet amazingly quickly it was incredible–I was thinking 'holy shit!' Everything was smooth; the canopy is out round your head; visibility is excellent.

W— Despite that big elliptical wing?

P—Well admittedly there's much more of it in front of you than in the Hurricane so the view downwards is a bit restricted. (At this point the interview is interrupted for a few minutes by the Boss and Jerry making a scramble for the beer.) Stalling (the point at which the wings stop producing lift)–very light, I did a few turns and it was really nicely co-ordinated, in fact to start off with I was using too much rudder, because generally speaking you need some rudder to roll vintage aircraft. But with the Spitfire when you start the roll it's balanced and you feed in the rudder afterwards, maybe it was the way I was flying it, but that was how it appeared to me.

W— When you put it into a turn do you need to put rudder with the turn or opposite rudder?

P— I don't know really. I found with the Spit that you roll in but initially it stays well balanced. What do you think Slam?

Slam— The thing that will cause you to need rudder is that when you have the angle of bank on the pitch will change because of the large gyroscope at the front (propeller). With the Merlin-engined Spits you'll need to correct the pitching tendency with left rudder. Conversely on take-off you need right rudder trim to counter the torque. With the five-bladed Griffon-engined Spits you need lots of right rudder. The gyroscope effect is very severe with the later marks.

W— I bet that was just what went through Paul's mind when he took off. He was thinking gosh what a big gyroscope! (everyone laughs)

P— I didn't have time to think about it. The aeroplane got off the ground so quick! All I thought was 'Oh my God!' Anyway at 7,000 feet I did a clean stall first nothing marked at all. (Interview is interrupted by an argument on who's going to buy the beers in the bar, and Sue Gardner calling–Shaaaagggger!)

Shagger—what a nice nickname that is! Tell Warren why I'm called Shagger then Sue! Be honest about this!

Sue—Because he was soooo good!

P— No it wasn't! It was because I kept breaking the bloody Chipmunk! Or rather the Chipmunk kept breaking on me! When I first joined the Flight everything I touched broke!

Sue—Yeah the Chipmunk went US for about a month after you'd used it!

P— And every airshow I was involved in was in appalling weather. When we did the AOC's (Air Officer Commanding's) checkout we started in a thunderstorm!

Sqdn Ldr Groombridge— Congratulations son. Have a beer on me.

P— Cheers Boss. (Boss ambles off out the door)

W— Right back to the interview. So what's the difference between a clean stall and a dirty stall?

P— A clean stall is with the undercarriage and flaps up. A dirty stall is with everything down. All of which was fine. The Spit buffets when it stalls and it dropped the left wing, but not violently or anything like that. And then I set the power to display setting and shot off down the hill and got to 270 knots just like that! Absolutely amazing! Took a few deep breaths and did a couple of practice displays for some farmer. Which must have surprised him, probably rang up and made a noise complaint. Then the Lancaster and one of the other Spits and Hurricane turned up and weren't polite enough to keep out the way. Zoomed back here to Coningsby.

W— That display you did here, was there a reason for that other than for the hell of it?

P— Yeah, that was for the benefit of Paul Day who is Fighter Leader. He cleared me for display, so now I can fly the Spit at airshows. Mind you, it wasn't a tidy display by any means. I was misaligned and I pulled up late for the victory roll because I bloody forgot! I was tootling along the runway at 500 feet thinking 'God, this is fun!' Saw the control tower approaching and I thought 'Damn I'm supposed to do something now–Oh yes!' So I pulled up and rolled–it was a bit late really, but so what. Then it was 'Oh shit–I've got to land the bastard now!' (Laughs)

W— Did you plan to make all those approaches before you finally landed?

P— I planned to do two rollers and a full stop. The first approach I rounded out far too high and pulled the power back too late probably because the Hurricane is three feet higher than the Spit. The second approach I was again far too high, so I just put the power back on and went round again. You may have noticed that I put the power on too quickly and the Merlin went bang before picking up. The third approach was better, held her off gently then once on the ground I pulled the flaps up and taxied her in.

W— So did your first flight in a Spitfire come up to expectations?

P— Yes, most definitely! It was fantastic! I think like many things you do for the first time it's fraught but even so the Spit felt right and as I become used to it, that feeling should get better and better.

Below–'Phew!' With obvious relief and a happy smile Paul climbs out of the 'baby' Spit after a successful first solo.

Above–Helmet still in hand Paul signs the aircraft log before disappearing with Sqn Ldr Day for a de-brief.

W— Will going back to flying Tornados ever feel the same again? Will you ever be able to enjoy flying F3s from now on?

P— Yeah because it's nice to occasionally get airborne and not feel completely panicky about it! (Laughs again). So that's about the size of it really!

W— I guess your first impressions must be pretty similar to how every pilot who's first flown the Spit must have felt since the prototype in 1936.

P— I guess so, although they probably weren't as concerned about the landings as I was. You hear all these stories and you get really concerned about doing the landing.

W— I suppose there must be a lot of pressure on you because you're flying such a rare Mk II Spit and you don't want to break it.

P— No, that never crossed my mind. Not at all. I'm always going to do my best to keep the bugger in one piece, but if it came to the crunch, then I'm afraid I'm more important that the aeroplane.

W— Which is the way it should be. Flying warbirds is a great thrill and privilege, but it should never be a risk to your life. Did you feel under pressure because Paul Day and everyone on the Flight was watching?

P— A little bit I guess. I had visions of them all standing there and saying–'Oooh he doesn't want to do it like that!' But as Jerry said when you're displaying you take no notice of the crowd. You just want to fly safely, that's what really matters.

Sue— Anyway Shagger, you looked great!

W— Well I think you're an ace mate. Congratulations!

P— Thanks very much

Right–Time for a laugh and a joke Paul takes a ribbing from Squadron Leader 'Uncle' Chris Stevens over his BBMF nickname of 'Shagger'. Happily Paul didn't break anything this time!

Throughout the summer of 1995 Paul Shenton found his every move followed by a cameraman making a documentary for the 'Discovery' channel. The attentions of the lens and microphone weren't always appreciated. Sticking your camera lens in the cockpit when the pilot is trying to go through their pre-flight checks is not a good way to make friends. Paul's first solo in the Spitfire was filmed from start to finish by the freelance cameraman adding to the pressure.

Above–At the end of a long day's work the BBMF groundcrew take a well-deserved break in the summer sunshine. Not a pretty sight! The groundcrew and pilots of the BBMF enjoy a relaxed informal relationship that is rare in the RAF in general. It's quite common for everyone to share a few beers after a long day.

Above–Groundcrew team portrait, some time during the long hot summer of 1995. From left–Sgt Paul Blackah, JT Tim Coulson, Cprl Fiona Holding, SAC Dave Ford, Sgt Keith Brenchley (who took many of the air-to-air photographs in this book), Cprl Simon Hingley and Cprl Wayne Martin.

Below–Cprl Druid Petrie grins at Flt Lt Jerry Ward as the Dakota ZA947 taxies out to the runway with a full load of VIPs. The relationship between officers and the technicians is relaxed and informal, far more so than is the norm in the rest of the service. However, the relaxed atmosphere does not effect the standards of workmanship and each member of the groundcrew takes a special pride in their work.

Above–Squadron Leader 'Slam' Allan Martin climbs into the Hurricane prior to another display in August 1995. 'Slam' flew in the fiftieth anniversary VJ celebrations. He described flying the Spitfire along the Thames in the evening flypast as 'The most fun he's had in a *very* long time!'

Below–Biggin Hill airshow June 1995. Are our intrepid aviators watching the flypast of an Su27? Left to Right–'Uncle' Chris Stevens, Bob Butterworth, Paul Shenton, Dave Ford and 'Nosey'Dave Parker. Actually, everyone is carefully listening to the radio in the BBMF road show vehicle. England was playing in the Rugby Union World Cup quarter final in South Africa. In the closing minutes Rob Andrew kicked a goal and so defeated Australia. To the obvious delight of everyone. Well, you have to get your priorities right!

CONCLUSION

The long hot summer of 1995 will be firmly entrenched in the memories of many. In years to come the apparently endless sunshine and blue skies will be remembered as halcyon days possibly never to be repeated. For me it was a period of exploration, of realisation of childhood dreams. For the Battle of Britain Memorial Flight it was the culmination of years of hard work by many, many people with a single goal–to ensure that there were airworthy aircraft to represent the Royal Air Force's 'finest hour' flying in the fiftieth anniversary celebrations of the ending of the Second World War.

Without the foresight of those who rescued the 'Last of the Many' from the scrap yards of a Britain bled dry by years of war and hardship, tears of remembrance and sighs of joy would not have greeted the song of Merlins. If you had said to the original members of the Historic Flight at Biggin Hill back in 1957 that their charges would still be flying in decades to come, they probably wouldn't have believed you. It is a tribute to all those people who have helped keep the aircraft of the BBMF flying since 1957 that a Royal Air Force Hurricane, Spitfire, Lancaster and Dakota were able to take part in the numerous Flypasts of 1995.

I'll never forget my flight in PA474. It is indelibly etched in my mind. As a glider pilot, I've flown more times than I can remember and only a few flights can be described as 'unforgettable'. I'm pleased to say that my flight in one of only two airworthy Lancasters in the world is noted down in my log book with the simple note–'Blimey!'

More than anything, though, what will stick out in my mind in years to come were the friends I made whilst researching and writing this book. It's no exaggeration to say that without these people, the aircraft that sit in the BBMF hangar at RAF Coningsby would be no more interesting than dusty museum pieces. It is the people and the way in which they interact with these aircraft of a bygone age that brings everything to life. Without even realising it the members of the BBMF have recreated the atmosphere of an operational wartime squadron right from the swearing warrant officer, to the pipe smoking CO. What is it about these aircraft that does that to people? I guess we'll never know.

148

Now that the fiftieth celebrations of the Second World War are over, it would be very easy to think that there is no real need for the BBMF anymore. You could argue that it has done its job, it kept the old warbirds flying for fifty years after the end of hostilities. Perhaps now is the time to let them retire–permanently. Surely now that the VE and VJ celebrations are nothing more than memories, interest in these old relics will fade?

I'm sure that as you read this now, there is some accountant in Whitehall looking at the estimated £1 million it takes to keep the BBMF running each year and shaking his head. In these times of defence cuts can we really afford such a luxury?

My own feelings are that paradoxically the BBMF is needed now more than ever. The world has become a very uncertain place. Old enemies have become new friends, whilst old allies have become enemies. Political idealism has been replaced by consumerism in one part of the world, whilst radical religion has replaced common sense in another. Let's face it—nobody knows where they stand anymore. Until recently the equation was simple, East versus West. Now? Who knows?

In some ways you can compare these uncertain times to the years leading up to 1939. Now, as then, many are suffering economic hardship. There seems to be a lack of political will in our own government and Europe is in turmoil once more. However, there is one major difference between the present and the past. The pre-war government saw the writing on the wall and halted the gradual erosion of the armed forces. This certainly isn't the case at the time of writing. The 'peace dividend', the result of the ending of the Cold War has led to huge cutbacks in all the armed services. The Royal Air Force is suffering as a result; moral has reached rock bottom. It seems to me that the squadrons are facing constant pressure to cut costs. There doesn't seem to be much faith in the Tornado as a fighter-interceptor, a role it was never originally designed for. Training is being cut back, reducing the number of flying hours among aircrew and holding back new pilots. Two of the BBMF's roadcrew for the 1995 season, Sue Gardner and 'Nosey' Parker found their training programmes cut and delayed. Other members of the BBMF are sadly looking towards civilian life for their future careers. By the time you read this, many of the faces in this book will have already gone.

In such uncertain times, it is vital to remember what the RAF is all about–the defence of this country regardless of the odds. This is what the BBMF does, it reminds us all, both those in the services and the general public, of a time when we knew who the enemy was; of a time when everyone was unified in the struggle to defeat regimes that were clearly evil; of a time when we cheered our heroes. In our present world it's like the song says there are 'no more heroes anymore'. The BBMF reminds us of a time when the heroes and heroines on all sides were too many to mention.

In a world with no clear future the roar of a Merlin engine helps to focus the heart and soul. Without the old warriors of the sky and those who tend them, you remove that point of focus, that reminder of a harder, but possibly more noble time.

If you try and erase the past, you are destined to repeat it.

Warren James Palmer
December 1995

149

first saw the BBMF flying at an air display in 1974, almost thirty years after the end of World War II. I remember thinking then that it was incredible that these old warriors were still flying and it would be a sad day, surely not too far in the future, when these vintage aircraft were finally grounded. All these years later the BBMF are still flying their Lancaster, Spitfires and Hurricane, a fact that seems incredible to me, not because the aircraft weren't well built originally, but because during wartime they were never designed to last more than a few months, let alone decades!

Today, over fifty years after the end of the war the imagination of small boys is still fired by their father's enthusiasm to show them pictures or models of Spitfires, Hurricanes and Lancasters, by way of introduction to the wonderful world of aviation. When you consider that most of these fathers were born in the sixties it's proof of the ageless attraction of these classic aircraft. I'm trying to picture the same scene in 2050; father saying to his small boy in reverential tones, 'Ah yes son, it's a Tornado'. I can't quite picture it myself. I'm willing to bet that there will be more Spitfires flying in 2050 than Tornados. They may be replicas rather than originals but who cares?

There are very good reasons why it's the aircraft of the BBMF which need to retain a very special status. Hopefully, if you've read this book you'll understand why. This book is a tribute not only to the aircraft but to the people involved in keeping the old warriors flying. From the less public faces of Yvonne and Ted, the mechanics and technicians, to those who are given 'star' status as aircrew at numerous airshows throughout the display season. It's a tough job, but someone has to do it!

It is a common supposition that the BBMF is run as a full squadron in the same manner as the Red Arrows. That isn't the case; the BBMF is run by a small team of engineers and staff. The aircrew are all part-time volunteers–the current day 'few'. For all the pilots it means giving up most of their summer weekends for the next three years.

Just seeing the aircraft of the BBMF flying together in formation at an air display can be a tremendously moving occasion. It's almost strange, there you are with possibly tens of thousands of other people on a hot summer's afternoon, not exactly over-come with emotion, but...affected by their display, like ghosts from the past. There's just something about them.

During the research for this book Warren and I have been given, most graciously, unlimited access to the aircraft, which on close inspection appear so vulnerable, particularly the 'baby' Spitfires. They're extremely small. My overriding impression is that unlike most of today's new designs, the aircraft of the BBMF were born of hand and eye, paper and pencil. There was a lot of human intuition and instinct involved in designing and building those aeroplanes. Perhaps that goes some way to explaining the strange affinity many of us feel towards these aircraft despite the generation gap; a gap between the past and present that grows with each passing year.

The reasons for the existence of the BBMF are like most things, arguable and the voices of those arguing against its existence appear to be growing louder. For me, doing away with the Flight would be like saying, 'Right, no more paying last respects, no more funerals, just forget them. It was only peace and democracy they were fighting for anyway. What's the big deal?'

We live in a society which honours its dead, let's not move the goal posts now. It would be very easy to let some faceless person at Whitehall get rid of a living part of our nation's heritage. It is really the loud and visible support of the public which maintains the Spitfires, Hurricane and Lancaster. Long may the Battle of Britain Memorial Flight continue, lest we forget.

Neil Lawson
January 1996

North Weald in May 1995 was the location for an event never seen before—a formation Flypast of a Spitfire, Hurricane, Lancaster and two genuine Messerschmitt Bf109s. The Me109 'Black 6' based at Duxford and Hans Dittes 109 flown by Mark Hanna of the Old Flying Machine Company formated with the BBMF at the Fighter Meet. The 109s took up station on the Lancasters starboard wing and flew past the crowd line twice as a tribute to fifty years of peace and reconciliation.

For some the decision to put old enemies together in one formation was a controversial one. It must be remembered that during wartime these aircraft were bitter rivals. However, it isn't the first time that Me109s and Spitfires have flown together without firing their guns in anger. During the Israeli war of independence the fledgling Israeli Air Force operated both Spitfires and 109s.

As the unique formation flew down the crowd line the clatter of cameras was deafening. Political correctness certainly was not a concern of the thousands that recorded the event for posterity.

It is a sign of the times that old scores are forgotten and people's sheer enthusiasm for classic aircraft replaces a need to relive old battles. As years go by and more and more rebuilt warbirds take to the air it will be these love for classic aircraft that will be the driving force that keeps them airworthy. The BBMF will undoubtedly find it's role changing in years to come but it is to be hoped that as part of the British Heritage, they will keep flying well into the next century.

Below–Messerchmitt Bf109s 'Black 6' and 'Black 2' formate on the Lancaster's starboard wing at the Fighter Meet at North Weald in May 1995. The 109s were flown by Mark Hanna and Dave Southwood as a tribute to fifty years of peace and reconciliation.

Opposite–On the evening of 6th May 1995 over 100,000 people packed into London's Hyde park for a VE-Day celebration. Lancaster PA474, Hurricane PZ865 and Spitfire AB910 made two flypasts. As nostalgic wartime songs boomed out from the stage the BBMF loomed into view and the entire crowd rose to their feet clapping, cheering and waving. The crowds outside Buckingham Palace were almost as big as those on the original VE-Day in 1945.

Lancaster PA474 performed a 'poppy drop' over The Mall in London on the fiftieth anniversary of VJ day. The mass of red is thousands of paper poppy petals falling from the Lancaster's bomb bay.